THE
ARTIST'S
OWN
BUSINESS

by
Calvin J. Goodman

Third Edition
Revised
&
Enlarged

Order additional
copies from:
Gee Tee Bee
11901 Sunset Blvd., 102
Los Angeles, Calif. 90049

TABLE OF CONTENTS

Introduction

This text is a distillation of the thousands of hours I have spent with artists, art students, and art dealers talking about their own business problems. I find it strange that the fundamental issues considered in these pages, while very much on the minds of many contemporary artists and gallery owners, have not previously been discussed systematically by specialists in business management. I have tried to bring to this work my own rather extensive professional experience and training in marketing analysis, promotion and sales methods, pricing policies, and dealer relations as they apply to the affairs of the artist and the art gallery operator.

For many years, I have been a consultant to businessmen in a wide variety of fields. In the past eleven years, my work has happily included advising many fine artists, artisans, managers of professional art workshops, and art dealers.

In addition, I have taught business methods and marketing courses to artists and art dealers at California Institute of Arts (Chouinard), Otis Institute of Arts, and Tamarind Lithography Workshop.

I have also conducted seminars and lectured to artists and art students in many organizations and communities, including Scripps Graduate School of Art, Silvermine College of Art, Artist's Equity of New York, University of California (Irvine), and California State College (Los Angeles). This revised and enlarged text arises out of these seminars, classes, lectures, and from my studies and actual experiences working with professional artists and their dealers. It is my hope that this book will be of immediate, practical value to other artists and art dealers.

Aside from the business methods and principles discussed here, one theme runs like a crimson thread through my thoughts on these issues: The artist cannot afford to adopt a romantic view of his financial problems, hoping to be "discovered" by a benefactor who will resolve all his economic difficulties, leaving him free to make art. He must vigorously seek out collectors who may be interested in his images. He must independently cultivate a following which is peculiarly his own. Everything depends on his willingness to work actively in behalf of his own career.

Calvin J. Goodman
Los Angeles, California
90049

THE DO-IT-YOURSELF APPROACH TO MARKETING ART

Why Should the Artist Market His Own Works?

Artists enjoy receiving -- and often actually
need -- the income as well as the gratification which
derives from the sale of their works. Although an
artist may consider the business scene distasteful,
even distressing, a negative attitude towards
commerce can make it exceedingly difficult for the
artist to function in his chosen profession. Unless
he has established another income source, he must
find a way to sell his works to collectors to support
his chosen mode of expression.

Of course, a well-established artist -- one with
a substantial following of collectors -- will have
relatively little difficulty enlisting the services
of an art dealer to sell his works for him. Some
artists even manage to place their works with a
number of dealers, thus achieving distribution in
several different market areas. Since dealers are
specialists in marketing art work, they are often more

capable of finding collectors and selling works than most artists can expect to become. Furthermore, they may experience less constraint in praising an artist's work or in encouraging a collector to buy.

Nevertheless, the relatively-unknown artist and the artist of good reputation but small market must find his own collectors. This may seem an onerous and even an embarrassing task, but there is seldom any other way for an artist to develop a significant number of collectors who are devoted to his work. First, there simply are not enough qualified art dealers operating today to handle all the good works which our better artists produce. I believe that the United States could profitably support twice as many first rate galleries as currently exist. But they are not appearing.

Further, most art dealers prefer to represent artists who have already achieved broad critical recognition and who already have a substantial number of clients. This leaves the excellent, but lesser-known artist to his own devices. He soon discovers

that he must sell his own work if he is ever to
achieve any recognition, reputation, or compensation
for his labors.

The encouraging truth is that selling art works
is not as complex as it seems at first. Indeed, a
few artists I know have mastered the craft of
marketing so well that they prefer to continue
selling their own works directly to collectors, even
after they are so well-established that dealers are
anxious to handle their works for them.

Some of these artists believe that they can earn
more money by selling their own works, retaining the
dealer's share of the price. It is unlikely that
this is true. In most cases, the effort required to
cultivate collectors and sell works of art necessarily
reduces the energy otherwise available to create new
works.

Few artists are so inexhaustible in their resources
that they can continue for a long period to do a wholly
satisfactory job of creating a substantial output of
works of art while simultaneously selling them at a
good rate. As a general rule, an artist should sell

his own works only until more efficient distribution
channels become accessible to him. He should then
find the best art dealers he can locate and turn
over the bulk of the marketing task to these specialists.

The artist should appreciate, however, that there
is a social aspect of selling his own work which is
rather important, aside from the monetary significance
of the effort. Every artist is, in some sense, a
communicator. Often, for the visual artist, this
function involves non-verbal communications -- an
effort to reach directly to the viewer's viscera or
to impinge somehow upon the viewer's sensibilities --
without recourse to written or oral language.

When the artist takes the trouble to study the
way prople respond to his work, to listen to their
carefully considered reactions, he can learn a
great deal about how his effort is succeeding. He
may -- if he is astute and open-minded -- even discover
aspects of his work which were not in his own consciousness when he was creating it.

Thus, showing, discussing, selling one's own work can be useful to the artist in more than a financial sense. It can improve his understanding of what his work is really achieving. I do not believe, however, that the artist can ever benefit from "explaining" himself or his work to others. Collectors may sometimes need a little clarification, guidance, or encouragement, but pat explanations cannot substitute for the collector's personal esthetic experiences.

Establishing a Reputation as an Artist

Before the artist can expect to sell more than a handful of his works, he will need to devote some energy to the establishment of his professional reputation. Credentials are important in all professions, particularly to that large class of clients who seem to trust the judgement of others more than they trust their own. To acquire these credentials, a capable artist needs only to exhibit his works widely under appropriate auspices.

The artist may enter his works in group shows, especially shows which are juried by well-respected connoisseurs and critics. He may also enter any of the numerous competitions which are advertised and available to relatively unknown artists. The magazines Art News and American Artist regularly list such competitions, well in advance of deadlines. Freight companies which specialize in crating and transporting art works also publish lists of exhibitions which are open to artists. The names of such companies can generally be found in a large city's Yellow Pages and in the advertising sections of the major art magazines.

Successfully entering shows and competitions will accomplish two ends. First, it will lend prestige and authority to the artist's implied claims that his works are unique, interesting, or note-worthy. Second, it will bring his work and his name to the attention of many people in the art world, including critics, dealers, and collectors --

many of whom visit these shows to view the works which are displayed.

Some artists feel that submitting their work to a jury or a committee in some way acts as a brake upon their creative freedom. This may be true. But an artist who is not well-known and is unwilling to participate in juried shows and competitions must achieve recognition in other ways. He might avail himself of the assistance and advice of friends who are already established in the art world -- other artists and collectors. He should realize, that even connoisseurs are often unsure of their own judgment. They tend to rely upon the testimonials and recognition of juries, prize committees, well-known critics, other connoisseurs, and other artists. Even very advanced collectors often seek assurances from others to reinforce or validate their own point of view.

While it is important that the artist enter shows and competitions, doing so is not inexpensive.

Usually, works must be matted or framed before they may be submitted. In many cases, an entry fee is required, which is not returned if the work is rejected. Also, the awards and purchase prizes are not necessarily commensurate with the market value of the work so honored. If an artist spends five dollars on an entry fee, thirty-five on a frame, twenty-five for crating and shipping, and then is "fortunate" enough to receive a two hundred and fifty dollar check for a work which has a fair market value of five hundred, he should realize that he has actually incurred an operating loss on the transaction. This loss may or may not be offset by the increased prestige and collector interest which the award arouses in the artist's other works.

Many well-established artists avoid competitions because they find that the economic disadvantages are not adequately counter-balanced by an improvement in their reputations or an increased exposure to collectors. On the other hand, juried exhibitions occasionally offer really attractive rewards, including more legitimate

prizes -- some of the best of these are not purchase

awards but simply honoraria -- good catalogues,

presitgious openings, and widely read critical

notices. Certain juried shows may even provide

good sales opportunities for the artist's works.

PROMOTION

Pre-selling the Artist's Work

Outside the art world, most products and services
sold to consumers in our fast-moving contemporary
culture have been at least partially "pre-sold"
before the buyer makes a purchase decision. A
sizable literature exists regarding the many subtle
and overt techniques which are employed to create an
awareness of a product's desirability and virtues
or to engender a favorable pre-disposition towards
or a reliance on a particular brand name.

Whether a potential customer is to be offered
a new automobile, an art work, or a new viewpoint
regarding our ecology, some organized force must seek
him out, gain his attention, and encourage a friendly
reception. These conscious forces, the advertisers,
taste-makers, and political leaders, are all
fundamentally promoters who use various communications
media to win adherents to their viewpoint.

Advertising and publicity are two different
varieties of promotion. The first is open and
purchased, the second is more informal and is not
always acquired for cash. Both are essentially pre-
selling tools. They may be employed with finesse
or crudely and still lead to great success. Or they
may be used so obtusely that the effort proves
counterproductive and destroys the very response
which the promoters were seeking. Promotional
efforts are extremely significant aspects of every
marketing endeavor.*

Successful promotion gives the prospective buyer
significant information. It stimulates a consciousness
of interest and need, encourages a positive attitude
toward purchasing, and informs the prospect regarding
his appropriate course of action. Large-scale
marketers of items intended for mass consumption
regularly spend a rather large portion of their
business incomes on promotion. One-fourth or more is

_____

*Marketing is sometimes used incorrectly as a synonym
for selling. It is, more properly the sum of several
activities, including promotion, research, planning,
pricing, and intelligence, as well as selling. Since
this is a specialized marketing text, each of these
functions will be examined in turn.

not uncommon. Only a few consumer products receive
limited promotion and still enjoy significant
acceptance in the market. (The Hershey chocolate
bar is a notable exception. This product enjoys
wide popularity with almost no promotion).

While the resources of the artist and his dealer
are generally too limited to permit large-scale
expenditures, the promotional problem of the artist
is not entirely unlike the problem facing many
producers of consumer products. The artist must
make potential clients conscious of the value of
owning art in general and aware of the existence of
his works in particular. He must also attempt to
favorably pre-dispose these clients towards these
works. And he must encourage the collector to
undertake certain expenditures -- to their own
mutual benefit.

But, there is also an important difference
between mass market promotion and promotion in the
fine arts. The artist seldom seeks or needs a large

market with vast numbers of collectors. More often, his images have a limited, highly specialized audience. Also his annual output is not extremely large. Further the appropriate clientele -- and the proper methods for reaching it -- for one artist can well be completely different from the clientele of another artist.

Thus, we cannot expect that the same promotional methods used to build interest in or preference for a particular brand of hair dryer could be directly transferable to the marketing needs of the artist. The pre-selling objectives of the artist and the art dealer are quite different from those of the mass market. The typical small appliance promotional program might be aimed at generating and maintaining wide-spread brand loyalty accross the nation -- plus a feeling of need for a particular contrivance.

But the promotional effort employed in interesting an individual in becoming an art collector in the first place, and the kind of publicity program which succeeds in stimulating a collector to take an active interest in a particular artist in the second place, must be much more precisely planned and aimed. Acquiring art is, after all, a highly individualistic affair. Of course, everybody "needs" art, probably a good deal more clearly than everybody needs a hair dryer. Still, not everybody can benefit from acquiring a certain work by a certain artist because not everyone has the same taste or sense of relevance. When we think of buying a work of art, popularity is not a primary factor determining our selection.

Pre-selling the works of a contemporary artist may involve: gaining recognition among a small group of specialists, achieving critical acclaim from a few critics or curators, collecting testimonials from these individuals in the form of remarks, purchases, or awards, and -- more important -- gaining a certain public exposure for these reactions, so that a some-

what larger group of collectors and others will
have the opportunity of learning that these events
are -- in fact -- taking place. Not everyone will
be equally impressed by an artist's work. Even
fewer will be moved so favorably that they develop
a pre-disposition towards acquiring a work. But
the artist's potential clients may be within this
group. If so, the promotional effort will be useful.

For example, suppose that a talented young
graduate of a professional art school submits a number
of his works to several exhibition juries. Suppose
further that some of these works are accepted. If,
in addition, critical reviews in the art press or
the metropolitan press mention these works favorably
and a few important collectors see and then acquire
some of them, or if a few works are awarded a prize
of some sort, then the artist's career has been
measurably promoted. His reputation is enhanced.
His future works are now, to some degree, being
pre-sold.

Now, further suppose that the community
newspaper serving the artist's home residence
runs a feature story on the young artist's recent
achievements. Clearly, this added exposure extends
that artist's "image" to a wider public. If
similar events occur in several communities or
in a major publication, then the "pre-selling"
is more wide-spread and a regional or national
market is possible. In this instance, promotion
is a function of communicating the facts about the
artist's growing recognition in such a manner that
the communication process itself contributes to
that growth.

For example, news items regarding events which help
to promote the artist's reputation include the winning of
a prize, the receipt of a commission, the announcement of
a one-man show, or the acceptance of an honor or a fellow-
ship.

How Can the Artist's Own Market be Defined?

But what causes these promotionally useful
events to occur? Different artists may employ a
wide variety of approaches, but the young artist
should not avoid the competitive, juried shows.
With all their limitations, such exhibitions are
an entry point for the little-known artist into
the art world. They can serve the same basic function
employed by the artist who encourages one-man or
group exhibitions in his dealer's gallery -- they
call attention in a meaningful way to the artist's
image. For the artist who lacks a dealer, a studio
sale can accomplish the same objective as a one-man
show.

Many artists believe that they must "innovate"
in order to attract attention to themselves. Others
prefer to adapt their talents to "popular" or
"acceptable" themes and styles. Viewed by themselves,
both of these approaches are wrong. The artist should
neither innovate just to attract attention nor follow
the fashion of the day just because it enjoys ready

acceptance. He should, of course, try to develop his own style and image, equally independent of fashion and the compulsion to be different. If the work is honest, well-done, and esthetically interesting, a market of its own can be found for it. The marketing problems of the artist consist first of identifying that objective market and then putting forth the promotional effort required to make contact with it.

An artist may find, as he studies his own work and talks about it with others, that his own community or circle of acquaintance does not contain sufficient potential clients for his work. He must then seek other areas of contact -- areas which contain his kind of collector. Art cannot generally be sold to non-collectors, no matter how well they know and like the artist, no matter how well his work is respected. So also, art of a particular medium, scale, esthetic bias cannot generally be sold to clients whose fundamental interest is pointed in a different direction.

Hard edge abstraction is of little relevance to
the householder whose home is a small museum of
authentic early-Americana. Apartment dwellers
have little opportunity to own a sculpture of
heroic dimensions. Not everyone relates to "magic
realism" in the same way. The artist must find his
own community of interest and then promote his
image accordingly.

Some artists may decide that their works are
primarily of interest to architects and builders
rather than to individual collectors, because of
factors of scale or subject-matter. Some might
conclude that their works will primarily interest
institutional and business collectors because of
their esthetic content. In each case, the artist
must define his own market. Where are the artist's
collectors likely to be found? What interests do
they possess? Why would they want his work in their
collection? These questions can seldom be posed
successfully before a body of work has been conceived
and executed, but they are very appropriate afterward.

Once the artist's own particular market is fairly well defined, he can better deal with the problem of reaching it. An artist who wants to devote a major portion of his life to creating large illuminated fountains must expect to gain little in the way of commissions from entering the local watercolor show. He needs to make contact with contemporary architects and commercial builders who might be able to integrate his fountain designs into their own structures. Further, his best clients will most probably be institutions rather than householders.

An architect might be expected to attend a competitive exhibition of sculpture or of sculptural plans, but he would probably not be found looking for talent at the watercolor annual. More concretely, an illustrated brochure or a portfolio of photos of maquettes, specially aimed at institutional architects, could be expected to produce a number of inquiries and even invitations for design proposals. But other promotional activity aimed at the general public or even at the home-oriented collector would fail.

Following the same logic, an artist whose images are rather conventional must realize that getting his work into a show at an institution which is well-known for its avant-garde viewpoint cannot do him any significant good. The collectors who may be expected to attend such an exhibition are not likely candidates to own this artist's work. They will come seeking something novel and challenging. They may even be offended by something which is merely pretty.

To summarize, pre-selling promotion is just as important to the artist as it is to the mass marketer, but it works differently. Each artist needs a small, specialized segment of the world's collectors for his following -- a segment which he does not share broadly with a large group of other artists. He must, therefore, seek a series of promotion-worthy events and activities which, by their nature bring him into focus in the eyes of just the right group of collectors for his images and in just the right way.

When Does Advertising Help the Artist?

Since advertising space is rather expensive, most gallery operators have apparently concluded that it should be employed sparingly and for informational purposes only. The use of purchased space in periodicals and newspapers seems almost entirely limited to terse announcements of names, dates, and places rather than to the more familiar advertising function of creating some sort of favorable pre-disposition in the client's mind regarding a product, personality, or cause.

An ad for a new musical play will generally feature selected remarks from critics who enjoyed the show. The basic purpose of this ad is to encourage increased attendance. Even the very august cultural establishments which sponsor symphony concerts and operas have begun to use advertising as a positive force to interest their clients in buying tickets rather than holding to formal announcements of coming events.

But the announcement of an artist's last
name in bold type, coupled with a gallery's name,
a date, and an address seems to encourage little
response. I am puzzled that gallery operators,
representing some of the most creative elements
in our culture, should be so consistently uncreative
in their advertising copy. They seem somehow to
have avoided the issue of why they are advertising
altogether. Thus, they seldom employ color although
this is a key to most of their artists' output.
And they have not found a way to utilize television
consistently although a work of art can be appreciated
visually more readily than verbally.

I look forward to the day when art is advertised
in periodicals and on television as effectively as are
other major elements of our culture, such as auto-
mobiles and political causes. One very appropriate
advertising approach would find art dealers banding
together to encourage more people to collect art --
to show them the advantages and tell them how they
might start a collection.

Gallery operators are more successful, and more rational, in producing direct mail brochures -- a form of advertising widely employed to promote attendance at exhibitions and especially to promote crowded exhibition openings. I shall reserve my rather negative appraisal of the limited function of such activities for a more appropriate place in this text. For the moment, it should be noted that these brochures often achieve their simple objective. They do promote attendance at gallery functions.

Essentially, a direct mail brochure, whether employed by a gallery or by an artist in his own behalf, should include several important items of information aimed at achieving its end. All of the vital information should be presented, clearly and without too much verbiage. The artist's name, his gallery's name and address, if he has a dealer -- if not, his own address -- the theme of the upcoming exhibition, the dates of the opening and closing should all be set forth.

I feel that it is an error to include the
artist's complete curriculum vitae, interminably
listing schools attended, exhibitions held, and
collections containing his works. This information
is useful to the scholar and should be carefully
preserved for eventual use in catalogues of major
retrospectives, but it makes tedious ad copy.
Two or three well-written sentences giving the
highlights of an artist's career will be fundamentally
much more informative because they are more likely
to be read and remembered.

The brochure should also contain one or two
imperative or hortative statements; "Please drop in
to see this important showing," "Don't miss this
opening," or "Phone for an appointment." In addition,
it is very useful to include an illustration of the
artist at his work, or a picture of an actual work,
plus a critical comment attributed to a dealer,
the artist himself, a critic, or to some other
authority.

Although this brochure need not be expensively printed and produced full color, it must be legible, neat, and a credit to the artist in terms of the taste and quality it suggests. Since many collectors save these documents for future reference, it should always carry a complete address and telephone number, including mailing zip code, and telephone area code.

Some artists will intentionally avoid any specific dates on their brochure so that they may use it extensively over a significant period. In this case, an added card or letter may be inserted in a mailing to signal a specific event. The brochure says something about the artist and his work. The card or letter says something about a specific event or opportunity. This technique illustrates the bimodal use to which advertising and publicity may be directed.

First, there is the immediate, <u>tactical</u> function of promotion. We wish to guarantee attendance at an opening. We wish to offer an opportunity to come, see, examine, buy certain works at a certain time. "Come to the opening." Second, promotion can have a more far-reaching strategic function. We want certain classes of collectors to be aware of an artist's existence and importance. "Ray Smith is alive and well and working very successfully in New York City." Or, we want collectors to be impressed with the growing acceptance of the artists' work. "Famous critic John Doe feels that Ray Smith's work is unique." In these cases we want a result of an intermediate, rather than an immediate nature.

It may not be as important that the collector come to a particular event as it is that he has a deeply-rooted, favorable view of the artist, his work, and his broad acceptance by competent critics and collectors. It is possible to produce an ad or brochure which aims at both tactical and strategic ends. "Come to the opening next Monday to see the works which John Doe finds so unique."

This simple statement joined to a familiar logotype and a recognizable signature works at many levels at once.

But, when the goals of advertising are not clearly set forth in the mind of the advertiser, his investment can easily be wasted. A full-page ad in a recent art journal illustrates this point rather well. The copy consisted of a large diagonal scrawl -- the illegible signature of a famous artist who was currently enjoying an important showing at a major gallery. The scrawl was recognizable to the cognoscenti, a handful of collectors familiar with the artist's signature as well as with the other pertinent facts of the case.

But the poor fellow who could not decipher the autograph, who did not know the unnamed dealer, or the dates of his show, was simply left out. Perhaps this was the real objective of the dealer, but he could have slighted his non-clients more easily and less expensively if no ad had been placed at all. An ad may be simple and direct or snobbish and sophisticated, but its purpose or purposes should always be clear to the reader.

How Does Publicity Serve the Artist?

Many business-oriented individuals think of publicity as a form of free advertising. Actually, this is not strictly true, first because it is not always without cost and second because, unlike advertising, the materials of publicity are not as readily controlled by their originator. Nevertheless, since the costs of publicity are more indirect and since the most familiar outlets for publicity are deeply interested in the work of fine artists, a good deal more energy is devoted by artists and art dealers to getting publicity than is devoted to preparing and placing advertising.

At its simplest level, the artist -- any artist with a noteworthy or amusing story -- writes a press release or gets someone to do it for him. The press release may announce a forthcoming or recent event of wide interest. Forthcoming events seem to be more important than those which have already occurred. Weekly publications need about ten days

advance notice to accomodate an exhibition opening
or a studio sale. A release might also announce
a recent award or a significant commission. The
main point is that information about the news
"hook" is furnished by the artist to the media --
not the other way 'round.

All good releases start by setting forth the
fundamental facts: who? what? where? when? why? how?

After a few leading sentences outlining the
anticipated or recent event in general, the press
release should go on to fill in details. A paragraph
on where and with whom the artist studied, some of
his major collectors, prior exhibitions, awards and
honors might be in order. Another paragraph
quoting the sentiments of a prominent curator or
collector might be employed. The closing sentence
might give a telephone number or an address where
further details are available.

The editor will decide whether the article is
newsworthy and will edit it to suit his interest and

the available space. Do not avoid giving the
whole story. The editor will cut out less
essential elements if he wants to do so.

This press release might be accompanied by a
glossy, 8 x 10 photograph of the artist receiving
an award, presenting a work, preparing a work in
his studio, smiling at a proud collector, etc.
Another photo might illustrate one of the artist's
works.

Care should be taken to prepare photographs
with adequate contrast to withstand the poor tonal
capabilities of most newspapers and many periodicals.
Light greys tend to vanish, while darker greys tend
to turn black. Fine lines often disappear entirely
in newspaper reproductions. Therefore, the artist
should not try to reproduce works with weak contrasts,
nor should he overburden a photograph with too much
detail. When individuals are present in a photo,
they should be accurately identified in a caption
taped to the bottom of the print.

A more advanced form of publicity is the feature
item. This is not an article based on a press
release, but a smaller item of interest to readers
and usually furnished to a columnist or editor by a
concerned individual. It might deal with an item
of news. More often, it deals with a matter of human
interest -- something noteworthy, amusing, or amazing.
Almost every publication carries some feature items
in a roundup column, generally written by a columnist
who may be specifically interested in art or
occasionally involved with cultural issues. Watch
these columns for examples worthy of emulation.

Magazines, Sunday supplements, and television
stations devote a fair amount of their resources to
public service and public interest subjects,
including the fine arts. A full-length feature
article or a television visit to an artist's studio,
a gallery, or a "happening" is almost always good
copy -- that is, the activity is new and unusual
enough to stimulate audience interest. Professional

publicists -- who generally identify themselves
as "public relations" consultants -- are often able
to develop good ideas for such features and special
programs. Of course, any imaginative individual
can, with a little thought, do the same. But try
to develop a feature concept in enough detail so that
it may be evaluated by an authority who knows little
about art.

Once a concept has been developed, it should
then be presented to the managing editor of a
periodical or to the program director of a television
station for his consideration. Where an influential
public figure -- a collector or architect -- is
involved, he may be the proper person to make this
presentation.

Features are also employed by specialized media --
the art magazines and the metropolitan newspaper art
pages. In these cases, the critics and editors who
select the materials are harder to reach because they
are literally inundated with suggestions and material

including proposals from powerful curators, advertisers, and collectors. Thus, they are the most difficult publicity channels in which one can make any progress.

Somewhat more accessible but often very important to the reputation of an artist are the metropolitan women's editors and their counterparts on the staffs of the women's magazines. Somehow the notion has gotten abroad that, since most purchasing in the United States is done by women, so too art -- culture in general, for that matter -- is a proper subject for women's pages and journals. I have no conclusive evidence proving that women do most of the art collecting and some evidence suggests that they do not, but nevertheless these are useful and prestigious avenues of publicity. A good proposal for a feature directed to the women's editor is likely to receive a sympathetic reception.

Again, however, as with advertising, it is possible to confuse ends and means in building a publicity program. If the end is a strategic enhancement of interest in an artist's general reputation, his image, his works, then it would be useful if these were represented to the kinds of people who can best relate to such works. These may be fashionable professionals or they may be underpriveleged youngsters. They might be architects or politicians. What counts most is the expression of interest and involvement of these specialized audiences. This interest is often much more important than the endorsement of a critic or a famous collector who has no peers and therefore sets no real patterns for others to follow.

The Great Dangers of Over-Promotion

Thus far, I have been discussing advertising and publicity as useful tools for pre-selling the artist's work. When they are properly used and directed, they can enhance the artist's career. But they are not always used in this straight forward manner.

Historically, and more particularly in the post

World War II era, certain collectors and dealers,

have discovered that great power and economic

advantage can be wielded by those who successfully

promote the careers of artists.

Accordingly, large sums are spent, sometimes

quite cynically, by promoters to bolster an artist's

name, image, and price structure. The mass media

and the major magazines are employed, in combination

with the antic efforts of friendly museum curators.

But, when these promotions succeed, and prices are

sufficiently inflated, the sponsors have a tendency

to "unload" their works on an unsuspecting public,

as tax deductible donations to museums, based on

current market prices. The promoters, having achieved

their own narrow ends, then withdraw their expensive

promotional support and go on to other artists where

the potential gain is still great.

Few artists can withstand the whiplash of a
meteoric buildup, followed by rapid withdrawal
of promotional support. They find themselves in
high fashion during a brief season and then quickly
the fad shifts and they are suddenly out of fashion.
The artificially stimulated demand is now gone and
the artist is suddenly left to his own devices.

A professional artist needs promotion, but not
the kind which builds his career too rapidly and
artificially and then leaves him dangling -- without
a valid constituency. The best promotional effort
is a carefully planned, deliberate program based on
finding real collectors, who will generally stay with
the artist as he matures and expands his and their
own experiences. Such a program underscores the
proposition that good art is never a series of passing
fads, but rather has the power to interest and attract
long after the movement of which it was a part has
lost its original novelty.

MARKETING PLANNING

The Importance of Carefully Planning the Artist's Marketing Activities

Properly conceived and executed, promotion is an important form of indirect contact with prospective clients. But, contacts with potential collectors must be only partially indirect. A direct approach can generally be more productive in terms of finding sales opportunities for artists. Towards this end, the artist, once he has initiated his "pre-selling" effort, must begin his marketing planning, an effort in which he seeks one or more avenues for frontal contact with potential clients.

Marketing Planning is a systematic, coordinated effort to establish prospecting and selling goals (coupled with promotional efforts) which are acceptable to the artist -- and to his dealer, if he has one. In planning his marketing efforts, the artist must also consider the methods which are to be used to achieve these goals and he should seek a way to measure the results which can be obtained through the employment of different marketing methods. Thus, marketing planning consists of setting realistic customer contact and sales goals, developing different methods of accomplishing these goals, and measuring the relationship between funds and efforts expended and results obtained through these different approaches.

Some artists feel that their market will (or should) develop more or less automatically -- without any planning -- as long as their works are interesting and properly priced. They assume that "somehow" their income from sales will eventually at least equal their expenses. This assumption, too often, proves incorrect. Many fine artists do not cover their own expenses with income from the sale of their works. In the last analysis, they support their art with funds obtained by working at other jobs or with income from other sources. Such artists are, in a sense, self-funded philanthropists. They are supporting their own work but gaining no significant financial benefits from the activity.

The artist (and his dealer) cannot generally afford a complacent attitude towards cultivating sales. At best, without planning, sales results will be erratic and difficult to anticipate. At worst, the lack of marketing planning can retard an artist's career and prevent him from ever reaching any significant number of his own potential collectors. To be sure, some sales may occur without planning -- or effort, for that matter. But one cannot live with the illusion that such sales will ever be a significant factor to the artist. They are fortunate accidents which only suggest how truly successful the artist might become if real planning were undertaken and followed by a vigorous marketing campaign.

Nor should one mistake marketing planning for business trend-plotting -- a common confusion among small businessmen. Business trend analysis is the study of external market factors which might justifiably

be considered by the artist, although such trends
are seldom directly responsible for his success
or failure. It is sometimes difficult to sell an
artist's work during periods of economic recession.
Also the waxing and waning of fashions in art may
notably influence an artist's fortune.

But good marketing planning can help the
artist and the art dealer to weather the vicissitudes
of shifting business conditions and changing vogues
among collectors. Such planning can even produce
sales results which are counter-cyclical so that
the artist's acceptance by collectors grows even as
business in general declines. This is possible
because many art collectors are free from the more
harmful effects of a recession and can move at will
into the art market to buy works, even when un-
employment is relatively high or the stock market
is bearish.

Incidentally, the most important long-term
market trend affecting the acquisition of contemporary
art in the United States is a very positive one. This

trend -- a very significant and continuing entry of
new collectors into the field -- is caused by a
general awakening of interest in what contemporary
artists are doing, coupled with a prodigious
growth in the number of families who have significant
discretionary income. Both factors date from the end
of World War II and show no signs of deteriorating.
They are particularly significant in that they
represent a relatively unsophisticated clientele.
That is, these new collectors and potential collectors
have the desire and the ability to buy art, but they
are not predisposed to a particular school or
esthetic bias. Their tastes can be developed in a
number of fruitful directions depending on who
reaches them and how their experiences are cultivated.

Relating Efforts to Success Rates

The basic assumption of the marketing planner
is that a measurable, reproducible, relationship
exists between the expenditure of time and money

on specific varieties of marketing activities

and the sales generated by such expenditures.

For example, we know that a well-written letter

of solicitation addressed to the right kind of

mailing list will produce a certain level of interest.

That is, one hundred personal letters to prospective

collectors, properly followed up with an equal

number of telephone calls will produce a given

number of opportunities to make sales presentations.

In my experience, the response varies between two

and ten percent, depending on the quality of the

letter and the list. A repetition of this same

kind of effort with a comparable list will, on the

average, produce the same rate of success.

Certainly, a well-designed letter directed to

a well-chosen list will produce better results than

a hastily contrived letter sent to a poorly selected

list. But, whenever the quality of the marketing

effort is held relatively constant, the number of

contacts and the volume of sales produced will depend

directly on the volume of solicitation and sales-

promoting activity.

The artist or dealer can discover, through

his own experience just how much of a particular

variety of marketing activity he needs in order to

generate a certain level of contacts or sales.

Of course, he may then improve on this ratio by

doing a better job within the marketing activity.

Better mailing lists, better solicitation letters,

smoother sales presentations will improve the rate

of success to be expected from any particular variety

of marketing activity. But, based on prior performance

and on anticipated improvements, it should be possible

to predict the sales results which a given level of

activity can produce over a given period of time.

Selecting a Variety of Marketing Activities

The artist and his dealer may engage in any

number of different activities aimed directly at

generating sales. For an artist at a particular

stage of his career and with a particular set of

opportunities and resources available, one combination

of these activities will be more effective in
advancing his sales than all others. As his
career develops and his opportunities and resources
improve, another combination of activities will be
more appropriate.

The most commonly used art marketing activity
in our culture is built around the one-man
exhibition of the artist's work. Publicity for such
exhibitions, the "opening" reception which is
generally held in conjunction with the exhibition,
and the show itself all serve to encourage potential
collectors to take an interest in certain works
which the artist has placed on display in the hope
that sales will be produced.

As suggested earlier, the exhibition will
generally lead to publicity. It is not hard to
use this activity as a device for promotion.
Whether it leads to any significant volume of sales
is another matter. I have talked with many artists
who were bitterly disappointed at the failure of

their one-man exhibitions to generate sales.

Through recent decades it has become fashionable to show only those of the artist's most recent works which pertain to a particular series. This fashion is very convenient for reviewing purposes, but it tends to violate the interests of any artist whose work contains more than one mood or interest. It certainly does little for the collector whose interests, biases, and needs are not served by the series placed on exhibition.

I seriously question whether this particular variety of marketing activity is effective enough to justify its being used almost to the exclusion of other approaches by artists and art dealers. For example, I find that group shows tend to produce more sales because they offer a wider variety of images to the public view. The contrasts are useful to the collector. Further, I find that artists' studio exhibitions and sales, which are generally not so specialized in their content, but tend to cover many moods and periods, are also more consistently productive of significant new contacts and sales.

Many successful dealers find that their best collectors abhor attending "openings," with their curious folkways. Thus, these collectors seldom buy at exhibitions. The dealers often justify their expensive, time-consuming, one-man exhibition programs on the grounds that "the artists expect it" and also on the proposition that "it brings new people into the gallery."

What the artist needs from his marketing effort, more than the prestige of another exhibition, is a consistent source of new and meaningful contacts and a regular activation of his established clientele. Further, there are many more productive ways of stimulating potential collectors to come into a gallery or to visit an artist's studio for the purpose of examining and buying art works. An impressive number of private dealers avoid the formal exhibition approach entirely because they find it wastes their resources.

The question remains then: is the artist's one-man, single theme gallery exhibition -- together with the publicity and "opening" normally associated with such functions -- an effective activity for stimulating sales? The answer seems to be that while it is a method which is widely used, it is often _not_ the most effective source of new or repeat sales available to the artist. Further, it should never be employed exclusively or even as a primary marketing activity.

The private sales presentation approach discussed more fully elsewhere in this text is probably the most effective method for making contacts, developing new clients and selling art works. This technique involves writing to a potential collector, sometimes enclosing a brochure, calling attention to the artist and his work, and inviting the collector and his spouse to a sales presentation at the gallery or at the artist's studio, where they may study the works in privacy. Unlike the formal gallery exhibition, where attendance takes on a social character all its own, at a private sales presentation, the prospective collector comes in for the specific purpose of making purchase decisions.

It is a consistently effective marketing technique, and a relatively inexpensive one, compared with the high cost of one-man exhibitions and their attendant publicity and opening costs. Further, unlike the exhibition method which requires an elaborate gallery exhibition facility, the private sales presentation method can be employed by anyone with a living room or a studio, including an artist or a private dealer.

Clearly, this method of promoting sales requires a certain amount of courage, since it puts the artist or his representative in direct face-to-face contact with relatively unknown, possibly even hostile, individuals. Further, in the case of some artist's images, and certainly in the case of some classes of mailing lists, one might find it necessary to exhaust a relatively large number of names before locating any qualified prospects. But once such a qualified prospect has been located, the probability of making a sale is rather high.

This solicitation and sales method requires a certain amount of market research to develop potential clients. One approach involves contacting members of a variety of professions -- law, medicine, dentistry, etc. -- in a particular community on the assumption that a fair percentage of such contacts will be interested in attending a private sales presentation. A more certain approach involves purchasing mailing lists of buyers of art books, subscribers to art magazines, members of arts associations, etc. for specific communities. Such lists are complied and sold by mailing list companies. The names of these firms may be found in the major metropolitan Yellow Pages listings.

My own studies show that artists and their sales representatives, working with contemporary works done by capable but relatively little-known artists in a wide variety of images can generally make a sale of one work per private sales presentation to a qualified prospect developed from such marketing activities. Thus, ten private sales presentations can yield an average of ten works sold, with an expenditure of considerably less effort and money than is required to mount a one-man exhibition, where fewer works are sold. Obviously, if the artist's reputation is better than average, if his image is more interesting, if his prospect lists and solicitation letters are better, then this success ratio can easily be exceeded. So too, if these factors fall below average, the artist may sell fewer than one work per presentation. Generally, results improve as experience is gained.

An interesting variant of this particular private sales presentation activity involves writing letters of solicitation to collectors who are already known to the artist or his dealer. It is far easier to write a letter or to make a phone

call to someone who has already done business with
an artist or his representative than it is to contact
someone who may not even have an interest in
collecting art works.

Of course, the easiest person to contact is
one who is already a collector of the artist's own
work. In this variant, the list of potential clients
is smaller, but the percentage of appointments which
can be made with such a list is greater. In any case,
the marketing activities involved in making appointments for sales presentations with old friends,
former clients,and those already acquainted with the
artist or the gallery involves a potentially much
higher rate of success than can be expected from
a similar activity with "cold" contacts.

Still another variant of this marketing activity,
which also leads to opportunities to make private
sales presentations, involves contacting collectors
who are referred or recommended by the artist's
clients and friends. A friend who is interested or
a client who is pleased with an artist's work may --

generally only when asked -- suggest acquaintances

and business associates who might be interested

in becoming collectors of that artist's work.

Again, solicitations where a referral exists are

easier to make. And they will probably produce

more private sales presentation opportunities

per hundred contacts than can be anticipated from

an equal number of "cold" contact solicitations.

In other fields, vast sales empires have been erected

almost entirely on the principle that referrals from

satisfied customers make the best prospects for new

business.

All of the above suggests that, as the artist's

clientele becomes more accustomed to buying his work

and, as the reputation associated with an artist

becomes better established, it is progressively

easier to make appointments to show and sell the

artist's work. Unfortunately, many artists and

their dealers -- through a curious combination of

indifference, cowardice, and sloth -- tend to relax

their efforts too early in an artist's career,

satisfying themselves with a modest, regional
clientele when much broader marketing opportunities
are available to them.

Thus, they tend to avoid actively seeking new
referral contacts; they give up entirely on "cold"
contacts and wait patiently for old clients to
come forward on their own. When such trusty, old
friends do come forward, they may be shown only the
artist's most current work. We forget the fact that
often the greatest interest of certain collectors may
be in an aspect of the artist's work which no longer
excites the artist himself. These earlier works
which the loyal old collector likes so much may now
be consigned to a dusty storage place where they
are inaccessible and largely unsalable. Realizing
the latent opportunity for developing new clients
and new markets or for stimulating old clients to
make new acquisitions can be hard work. As a result
of their failure to do this work, many fine artists
reach only a small portion of their potential market.

Some artists create works which are of a scale, nature, or medium that suits them not for a private home but rather for a public place. A new office building, a newly furnished suite of offices, an outdoor shopping mall, a branch bank all are excellent prospects for institutional purchases of art. Here, the appropriate solicitation lists consist of architects, builders, decorators, and designers, rather than professionals, art magazine subscribers, and art book buyers. One good source of prospects for such works is the "Green Sheet" or Dodge Report which lists new construction plans, describes their scale, and notes the architect in charge for each major community. Other lists, such as the rosters of the local architectural association or the designer's society, are readily available. Some of the best lists are available in the local Yellow Pages without cost to the artist.

How and When the Artist's Marketing Planning is Accomplished

An artist who is not represented by a gallery, or is only represented in certain limited market areas, should do his own marketing planning. Occasionally, he may call upon his spouse or a good friend for assistance and advice. Regularly, he should seek new list sources and revise his old lists. At least once every six months, he should replan his marketing activity for the entire year ahead, refining, reviewing, and finalizing those activities which lie within the six months just ahead and laying the basis for functions which require longer range planning than can be accomplished within a six month period.

Planning should always be done with an eye to the practical experiences of the immediate past, as well as in terms of new opportunities for the future. The number of solicitations and contacts made, the results achieved from those contacts during the prior six or twelve months should not limit the artist's future plans, but they should certainly act as a guide in terms of what has been accomplished and what functions need improvement or reorganization along more effective lines.

Once a plan for the next twelve months has been finalized, a calendar should be established on which anticipated events and scheduled targets may be recorded. These should include dates for the development and completion of new or revised mailing lists, deadlines for the preparation or revision of promotional and solicitation letters, dates for mailing these letters and making follow-up phone calls, dates for the preparation of publicity releases, articles, and illustrations, deadlines for the development of brochures and catalogues, and for entries in juried competitions, participation in group exhibitions, and preparation of one-man shows and studio sales.

Where an event cannot be set down precisely in a timetable for lack of certain information, it should be listed to the side of the calendar and a deadline

should be set for finally calendaring it. Thus,
it may not be possible to say a full year in
advance precisely when a brochure will actually
be ready for distribution. But it should be
possible to determine that the design and
specifications for the brochure, the quantity to
be produced, its cost, and its date of publication
will have been determined no later than a specified
date, say three months hence. By that time, these
items should be ready for detailed and more precise
scheduling and budgeting.

Using the Marketing Planning Sheet

An artist who works in different media has different
sets of marketing problems. A separate form of the kind
shown on the next page should be used for each time
period planned and for each medium in which the
artist is engaged. A summary sheet may be used to
summarize the contents of each separate planning sheet.

MARKETING PLANNING SHEET

Use a separate sheet for each medium

Oils and Acrylics_____   Orig. Prints & Dwngs._____
Wtr. Colors & Collages_____   Sculptures & Assembls._____
Mixed Media_____

Sales Objectives:

_____works in this medium to be sold in this planning
period.
vs._____works in this medium sold in same period, prior year.
@$_____, average selling price per work in this medium.
vs.$_____, average selling price per work in this medium,
same period, prior year (up by ___%).

Success Ratio:

_____number of works expected to be sold per hundred
sales presentations.
_____number of works sold per hundred sales presentations,
same period, prior year.

Activity Rate:

_____sales presentations needed to achieve new sales
objective.
vs._____sales presentations actually achieved in this
medium, same period, prior year.

Solicitation Rate:

_____letters and calls needed to produce _____sales
presentations per period.
_____personal contacts needed to produce _____sales
presentations per period.
vs._____letters and calls generated for this purpose,
same period, prior year.
_____personal contacts made for this purpose,
same period, prior year.

Supporting Promotional Program:

Anticipated sales volume from this
medium, for this planning period: $_____

_____% of anticipated volume allowed
for advertising and publicity.

Total promotional budget for this medium
and period: $_____

59.

Where marketing planning is being done for a one-year period, three forms should be prepared for the artist's oils and acrylics. One of these covers the nearest three-month quarter, the next covers the second three-month quarter, and the third covers the last six-month period.

The artist should begin by filling in all the information which is already known, such as the number of works of this medium he has sold during the same period of time for the year which has just concluded. He should also record the average selling price per work sold in this medium during that period, the number of works of this variety sold per sales presentation made during the period, and the total number of sales presentations in which works in this medium were shown to prospects during the period. This information can be extracted from the artist's appointment calendar and from his sales invoice records. The latter will be discussed more fully later in the text.

On the summary marketing planning sheet, the artist should record the total number of contacts which were made for the purpose of making sales presentation appointments and the number of personal contacts made for the same purpose, together with the prior years' budget for advertising and promotion, figured as a percent of total sales generated.

If these historical figures are not available, it is probably because poor records have been kept and because sales efforts have been sporadic. Beginning with the first formal marketing plan, the artist should establish a simple calendar diary in which he records, as the events occur, the number of solicitation letters sent out on each day, the number of phone calls made, the personal contacts made, the number of sales presentation appointments made, the number of works sold at such presentations, as well as the value of the sales made. To make his marketing planning even more effective, the artist should summarize his actual experiences, weekly or

monthly, so that his performance and results may
be compared with his plans. As goals are realized
and expanded, their usefulness becomes clearer.
When targets are not being met, this should be a
spur to greater efforts and more effective work.

For example, consider an artist who sold $4,000
worth of art works, all of them oils or acrylics,
during the course of the twelve-months which just
concluded. If that artist sold a total of fourteen
works, then his average selling price in this medium
was about $285. If he made a total of twenty sales
presentations (counting each effort, including repeats
to the same client) during the year, then he sold an
average of 14/20 or seven-tenths of a work at each
private sales presentation. This amounts to close to
three works sold for every four sales presentations
made. If this artist had sent out one hundred letters
and made one hundred phone calls to arrange the twenty
sales presentation appointments, then he must have sent
out five letters for each appointment made.

Now suppose that this artist is determined to improve upon his sales performance in this medium over the prior year by a factor of one hundred percent. That is, he has decided that he is ready to sell eight thousand dollars worth of his work in this medium during the next twelve months. This is not a difficult goal, but it requires consistent effort and good planning -- as well as an adequate and diversified inventory of works.

To begin, the artist should carefully consider his selling prices. He may decide that an average of $285 per work is no longer appropriate. If his prices were increased by an average of only five percent, he could be receiving an average of $300 per work. In that case, to generate an income of eight thousand dollars for the new year, he would need to sell about twenty-seven works.

It may be that this artist feels he can also improve on his success ratio. That is, he may be able to increase the average number of works sold per sales presentation. Certainly, as he gains experience and makes appointments only with fully qualified prospects (a concept discussed more fully in the section on selling), and as he makes better sales presentations, the artist can expect to sell more than three works for every four presentations. Some collectors will buy more than one work at a time. Old clients and referrals are more likely to buy than new contacts. My own "norm" is one work per private sales presentation.

But, to keep his marketing planning conservative, this artist may decide to base himself on his own older, proven success ratio. On the basis of history, he will need to make approximately thirty-six good sales presentations during the course of the year in order to sell twenty-seven works. Of course, if he actually manages to improve on his effectiveness in making these presentations, the artist will sell more than the targeted twenty-seven works. In that case, he will exceed his planned volume.

Next, the artist must determine the solicitation
activity level required to produce thirty-six private
sales presentation opportunities. In the prior year,
this artist found it necessary to send out five
letters and make at least five phone calls or
personal contacts for every sales presentation
appointment he was able to arrange. Again, it may
be that with superior letters, improved lists and an
increased level of referral business, as well as more
repeat contacts with his own established collectors,
the artist may find it easier to achieve his target
of thirty-six sales presentations in the year ahead.

But presuming that he can make no improvement in
any of these rates, he should schedule one hundred and
eighty (thirty six times five) letters and calls of
the kind he made in the prior year, as the solicitation
rate needed to produce thirty-six qualified sales
presentation opportunities during the year. The
artist now knows that the chances are very good,
that if he makes approximately that many solicitations
in the form of letters, calls and personal contacts,

he will, in fact, generate more than enough private

sales presentation opportunities and more than

enough sales to double his prior year's volume.

Next, the artist must divide this anticipated

marketing effort into smaller, more manageable,

time elements. The three month period which begins

in October and ends at the year end might reasonably

include thirty-five percent of the total planned

effort, since this is a major buying season. July,

August, and September might include only twenty

percent of the planned activity because summer

vacations reduce sales opportunities in this artist's

community. The remaining forty-five percent of the

plan could be divided equally over the remaining six

months.

The artist will, during all these periods, be

working almost twice as hard at showing and selling

his works as was necessary to generate the lower

volume of the prior year. Remember, however, that

as his reputation and effectiveness improve, it will

not take this much effort to maintain the same sales

level. Prospective clients will become easier to

reach and interest. But any significant new increase in volume level will require added effort because new clients will be needed.

Once the artist has decided that he can, in fact, produce eight thousand dollars in sales volume, through a specific marketing plan, he must then decide upon the advertising and promotion program which he can afford and which is appropriate to support this level of sales activity. Many successful gallery owners spend as little as three to four percent of their annual anticipated sales volume on promotion (not including exhibition costs). Where a radical change in volume is anticipated, a greater proportion might be needed for the desired result.

Suppose the artist in our illustration decides to set aside five percent of his anticipated sales volume for advertising and promotion. This means that he should plan to spend $400 during the course of the year. This sum might be spent entirely on

one or two brochures, illustrating the artist and
his work and containing a few significant critical
comments. Such brochures might be employed as
companions to the solicitation letters. Promotional
funds might, alternatively, be spent developing a
publicity program designed to get positive, critical
attention for the artist and his work in certain
local or national art publications. In this case,
the money might be used for high quality photographic
illustrations to be furnished, together with
appropriate press releases to the pertinent publications.

For example, the artist or his representative
might contact metropolitan publications to interest
them in running an illustration of one of his works
with a suitable credit line or caption. If the artist
supplies several different 8 x 10 black and white
glossies, this would be an appropriate promotional
expense. The preparation of color separations for
color illustrations is much more expensive. Several
hundred dollars might be required to produce just a
few properly corrected color separations to be used

in an art publication to illustrate the artist's
work. The artist might seek the assistance of an
art curator or a free-lance art critic in
preparing captions or comments for such illustrations.
Sometimes these specialists are paid for their efforts.

Once the artist has completed a marketing plan
for the quarter, half-year, and year ahead, he must
proceed to calendar the specific tasks related to
this plan. These include the preparation of
solicitation letters, mailing lists, etc. A list
of typical marketing tasks is appended in the
quarterly Marketing Schedule Sheet. This sheet
should be used as a graphic reminder of specific
tasks to be accomplished. The illustrated sheet is
designed to aid in accomplishing three months of a
marketing plan developed for the artist discussed
in this section. The reader, will, of course, want
to adapt the style of this sheet to his own purposes
and he will want to develop similar forms to cover
other time periods.

Time Period Oct. 1 to Dec. 31

QUARTERLY MARKETING SCHEDULE SHEET

Week Number

	1	2	3	4	5	6	7	8	9	10	11	12	13
a) Prepare-revise Mailing Lists	X	—	—	—	X	—	—	X	—	—	—	—	—
b) Prepare 63 Letters for Mailing*	—	21	—	—	—	21	—	—	21	—	—	—	—
c) Telephone Follow-up/Contact	—	—	21*	—	—	—	21*	—	—	21*	—	—	—
d) Make 9 Sales Presentations	—	—	—	1	1	1	1	1	1	1	1	1	—
e) Prepare Brochure Copy and Layout	X	—	—	—	—	—	—	—	—	—	—	—	—
f) Produce Brochure	—	X	—	—	—	—	—	—	—	—	—	—	—
g) Prepare Photo-Illustrations & Color Corrections	—	—	X	—	—	—	—	X	—	—	—	X	—
h) Prepare and Issue Illustrated Press Releases	—	—	—	X	—	—	—	—	X	—	—	—	X

*This schedule calls for a minimum of 21 letters and personal contacts per month, to achieve a total of 35% of the 180 solicitations needed per year. More contacts are permissable during this quarter, of course.

70.

Time Period _____

QUARTERLY MARKETING SCHEDULE SHEET

Week Number

	1	2	3	4	5	6	7	8	9	10	11	12	13
a) Prepare-Revise Mailing Lists													
b) Prepare ___ Letters for Mailing													
c) Telephone Follow-up/Contact													
d) Make ___ Sales Presentations													
e) Prepare Brochure Copy and Layout													
f) Produce Brochure													
g) Prepare Photo-Illustrations & Color Corrections													
h) Prepare and Issue Illustrated Press Releases													

71.

PROSPECTING AND SELLING

Contacting Prospective Collectors

Serious collectors and newcomers to the field share an interest in meeting "new" and "upcoming" artists. Many collectors find that the beginning of their interest in acquiring works coincides with an introduction to an artist. As any artist's recognition grows, he will experience a number of opportunities to meet collectors. These meetings might take place at a museum exhibition or at a reception sponsored by an art gallery in behalf of the artist himself or for another artist's work.

To meet potential collectors, the artist should learn to "swim in the waters" which art collectors and would-be collectors inhabit. An artist who regularly attends museum exhibition openings, gallery openings, and other social functions in the art world, inevitably encounters many collectors. Such opportunities abound for the artist who is judicious in the allocation of his time.

Collectors of many levels of sophistication may also be found in more prosaic walks of life. For example, the artist's attorney, doctor or dentist may be an art collector or wish to become one. The artist's friends or relatives may aspire to collect works of art. If the artist is also a teacher, he is likely to discover that some of his students and their families are art collectors. The circle broadens considerably when we consider the professional contacts, friends, and relatives of the artist's own friends, acquaintances, and relatives.

Once the artist begins to think in terms of entering the art market, he should inaugurate a card file, with a card devoted to every potential client he meets. On each card, he should note this contact's name, his wife's name, his residence and office address, his telephone numbers, and any pertinent information the artist may have learned regarding the esthetic interests of the collector and the preferences which that collector may have expressed for individual artists or their works.

This contact file should grow steadily as the artist's career develops. It will be a useful asset even after the artist has acquired satisfactory dealer representation and a substantial following. Even negative information can be useful. It helps the artist to avoid wasting his time on a non-prospect or curiosity seeker whom he has previously met.

As indicated earlier, there are many potential clients who are total strangers to the artist. Finding their names and addresses, finding a way to interest them in examining an artist's work is a matter of effort and energy. The supply of potential contacts is almost limitless. They must be cultivated by the artist or by his representative.

When the artist has developed a contact file with a hundred or more names, he is ready to begin soliciting for sales. This step may seem presumptuous, and bothersome -- even frightening -- to the in-experienced artist-salesman. It should not be any of these. The fact is that genuine collectors will usually welcome an opportunity to see an artist's works, especially if they have not previously been available to them and may contain surprising, interesting, or exciting new elements.

After all, it is only by viewing these works for themselves that collectors can determine whether they are really interested in them. It is axiomatic that if an art work is worth owning, it is worthy of being offered to the view of a prospective collector. As for the novice who is just learning to collect -- his need is greater, since his prior opportunity to study contemporary art has been necessarily more limited.

As suggested earlier, one simple technique for opening a sales campaign involves sending out personal solicitation letters. These should be typed on plain bond or on simple stationery. Generally, such letters indicate that the writer is an artist who will be phoning within a few days to invite the collector to a private presentation of his work, in the hope that one or more of the works shown might find their way into the collection of the potential client.

The letter might begin with this type of

opening paragraph:

Dear Mr. and Mrs. So-and-So:

When we met at the XYZ museum exhibition
opening last Thursday, you commented
that you were interested in seeing some
of my original art works. As I remarked
at the time, I work mainly in acrylics
and oil, although I occasionally also
create small sculptures.

An alternate opening might read:

Our mutual friend, Mrs. L.M. Enn,
recently suggested that you might be
interested in seeing some of the art
work which I have recently created.
As you may know, she owns two of my works.

A third alternative might begin:

You may not be familiar with my work
as an artist, but I believe you will
find it quite interesting and
provocative -- perhaps even worthy
of your own collection.

The letter could go on:

Although I am not currently represented
by any of the major art dealers, my
work has recently been exhibited at
the XYZ Museum's New Artists Show. I
was awarded a special purchase prize

at the ABC City Art Association
Show last fall. As a student, I
worked with several of the best
contemporary artists in this part
of the country, including J. Roe and
A. Smith.

Since I understand that you are
developing a collection which is
meaningful to you, it would make me
very happy to arrange a private
presentation of some of my works at
my own studio for some evening next
week, or for a Sunday morning, if
that is more convenient. I will
call you in a few days to make an
appointment. Thank you for your
interest and encouragement.

                    Very truly yours,

Once the artist has learned to develop his own

constantly-expanding contact list and has designed

his own solicitation letters, the task of systematically

sending out individually-typed letters and then

following them up with phone calls leading to

appointments should become routine matters. As

discussed earlier, a certain number of letters and

phone calls will yield a certain number of private

sales presentation opportunities. Continued effort

will yield continued results. Improved letters and

better prospect lists will yield even better results.

Some people will decline to visit the artist's studio simply because they are disinterested. They may be the majority of those contacted. Others will be interested but simply unable to arrange a convenient date. These should be calendared and followed up at a later time. Do not throw any contact cards away. A refusal or a postponement is not really the same thing as an outright rejection.

After all, these prospects have not seen the work. They may become more interested later on in the artist's career after they have become more interested in art or after they have learned from others about the interesting works they have been passing up. If the file cards are destroyed, the artist might forget whether he has previously contacted certain prospects. Or he may forget when the contact was made or what the response was. A renewed or different approach at a later date may prove more fruitful. Even the contact who seems negative or diffident at first may turn out to be a devoted collector.

I have never discussed this question with an experienced
salesman who took a different view. Every really
successful salesman knows that his best clients often
did not start out as friendly, receptive prospects.

Qualifying Prospects

Regarding the prospect who says that he is
interested in visiting the artist's studio, it
should be made clear to him that -- while the visit
may well be educational and pleasant -- it is aimed
specifically at selling art works. When first meeting
the prospect, and again when making an appointment
on the telephone, the artist should attempt to
discover whether the prospect already owns any
original art works. He might also discover the
names of the artists represented in the prospect's
collection and the type of art in which the prospect
is most interested. This line of inquiry might lead
to an opportunity for the artist to indicate that he
hopes to show the collector and his wife several
works which are "worthy" of a place in the prospect's
collection.

So too, the solicitation letter should mention
the fact that the artist hopes that some of his
work will find their way into the prospect's home
or office. If the collector does not clearly
appreciate the business function of his impending
visit, it might be necessary to expend a good deal
of energy simply "educating" him on the importance
of collecting. This is a worthy and socially useful
endeavor, but it is not the artist's primary consideration.

The question which must be answered is _why_ the
prospect wants to visit the studio. Is he a serious
collector or just curious about how artists spend
their time? The latter is really not a very good
prospect. In fact, non-collectors are generally poor
prospects unless they have recently decided to
become collectors -- usually a conscious decision.
Artists and art dealers should devote a fair amount
of time to finding and encouraging non-collectors
to join the ranks of the collectors. This is good for
art and for novice collectors as well.

But a private sales presentation is not the right occasion for such discussions. They belong in the lecture hall or at a public gallery. The private presentation is a formal sales situation. It should be accessible only to qualified prospects. When I have my choice, I do not like to even permit the prospect's friends to join him at such a presentation. They often spoil the mood of the occasion and interject irrelevant views and interests.

It is, of course, possible to sell art works under very informal circumstances to totally un-qualified contacts. But very few works will be sold this way because the circumstances are all wrong for the prospect to study and react to the work, for determining what the collector really wants, for helping the collector to make a positive decision. The best justification for private sales presentations is that they produce more consistent, more effective results for the artist and for his collectors.

When the collector and his wife arrive for
their appointment, after making them welcome, the
artist-salesman would be well-advised to "requalify"
his prospect by clearly restating the purpose of the
prospect's visit. For example, he might say,
"I feel sure that you will find these works of mine
interesting and unusual. I hope to be able to show
you several which belong in your own collection."
Alternatively, he might say "I remember that you said
you liked John Smith's work. While our works differ
a good deal, many collectors feel that my work is
comparable to his in several significant ways. I know
a number of individuals who prefer certain of my
works to any of his they have ever seen. But, I would
like your judgement about that."

By this point in the text, a number of my readers
may be objecting that this sales approach is crass,
commercial, brazen, or "pushy." I would like to
submit that the alternate approach to selling art --
to let the work "speak for itself" -- is _not_ more
polite. It is simply less productive. The artist

should certainly not be overly aggressive in presenting his work or in asserting its virtues. A high pressure salesman will often defeat his own purposes through his insensitivity to the needs and sentiments of his clients.

However, if the artist is to make any headway with a marketing program, he must take an _active_ rather than a _passive_ approach to his sales problems. Long ago, most merchants discovered that the world does _not_ beat a path to the door of the best mousetrap inventor without active stimulation, guidance, and encouragement. Certainly, in the field of art, clear pathways must be opened for the collector, or he will remain lost to the artist for all his _bona fide_ interest and good intentions. Few artists are ever really "discovered."

Making an Effective Sales Presentation

Before the prospective clients arrive, the artist should prepare a comfortable sofa or two separate chairs in a specially dedicated room or area of the studio. The seating should be placed at a suitable

distance from the exhibition easel. This should

not be the easel which is regularly used for making

an art work, as such easels require considerable

manipulation. More properly, it might be a

specially contrived display easel consisting of an

"A" frame, built of plywood and inclined about

sixty degrees from the horizontal plane.

Any artist who is handy can build his own

display easel. The "A" frame should have two sides

and may be mounted on casters. On one side, a ledge

should be located approximately thirty inches from

the floor of the studio. A similar ledge on the

other side may be located closer to the floor to

accomodate larger works. The easel's ledges should

place the center of attention of the work just a

little above eye level to the seated visitors. The

entire framework may be carpeted in a neutral

carpeting to serve as an inobtrusive background for

framed or unframed works.

Natural or artificial illumination should be directed at the work from the ceiling, well in front of and above the head of the prospective client. In this position, lighting will be most useful as neither the client nor the artist-salesman will cast his own shadow on the work itself.

In presenting art works to the prospect, the artist should avoid having too many works on casual display. None of these should be particularly powerful works which are not for sale. They will prove a distraction. The artist should not present more than one or two works at a time, and should keep the total number of works shown at any viewing well below twenty. Ten works, carefully considered is really a large number for an evening. Only experienced connossieurs can examine a larger number of art works without developing a good deal of confusion regarding the works which they have seen.

If the artist's works are three-dimensional or otherwise hard to handle, the artist might set them up on the floor, on pedestals, or on tables in various

parts of the studio, arrange appropriate lighting,
and then drape the works before the prospects arrive.
This arrangement heightens the prospect's
anticipation and sharpens his attention.

The greatest advantage of a private sales
presentation over a gallery exhibition is one of focus.
But the prospect's focus is diffused quickly if too
many works are on view at the same time. In this
connection, the Italian writer, Pavese, makes an
important observation regarding the role of the artist
when he proposes that the primary task of the artist
is one of focusing the attention of his audience on
his work in such a way that the viewer is made to
see it as if he had just discovered it for the first
time.

Having requalified the prospect and arranged
the viewing circumstances, the artist is now ready
to begin the next step of the selling routine. The
customer is present in the studio on a clearly
acknowledged business mission. It is now the artist-
salesman's task to see that he becomes personally

involved with the work which he is examining.
This involvement may or may not lead to a sale,
depending on the prospect's ability to follow and
the artist's ability to communicate -- first as
an artist and then as a salesman.

The first work is disclosed and mounted on the
easel. It need not be the most exciting or even
the most effective work on hand. It will be useful
in telling us something about the prospect's visual
equipment and esthetic bias.

One might start by asking the client to report
what he "sees" in a work. Remember that many in-
experienced viewers look only for subject matter.
They are often conscientiously blind to color, form,
composition, symbolism, technique, and other aspects
of an art work which may be very important to the
understanding of the work which has been shown.
Try to be patient with the viewer whose esthetic
and visual capabilities are not as well developed
as they should be.

Encourage him when he recognizes something
significant in a work. Guide him a little if he
seems confused or needs orientation. Sometimes
a hint or a leading question will be very useful.
Most collectors will appreciate a little help.
But, be careful. A more sophisticated collector
may feel patronized or "put down" if the artist is
too helpful. Do not offer more information than
the prospect seems to need and want.

Sometimes a client will ask an artist to
"explain" a work. Artists often take offense at
questions of this variety. After all, a work of art
should not generally need any explanation. Try to
encourage the client to "see for himself" what is
happening in the work. This can often be accomplished
by answering his questions with appropriate questions.

For example, the artist might reply, in truth:
"it is very difficult for an artist to properly and
fully explain his own work, except in visual terms.
Why don't you freely associate and tell me what you
find here on the canvas? Perhaps then I will be able

to tell you whether you see things the way I do or not."
Some artists might prefer to say: "I am not sure I
am always able to express my own views in words --
I often have difficulty verbalizing it. Perhaps
that's why I am a painter rather than a writer. Why
don't you tell me what you see? We may both gain a
better insight this way."

Of course, an artist's image often contains
political, religious, or historical references.
It may include symbolic references to cultural
developments or to the works of other artists.
Sometimes, the artist is visually commenting on
society or on his own environment. If the client
is astute enough to recognize such contextual
references, he deserves credit and encouragement.

In such cases, however, if he is not able to
recognize the subtler contextual implications of a
work, he may really need a little advice or a little
information. This could be done in a very general way,
as when an artist outlines his basic purposes or his

motivating interest in doing a group of works.

The artist cannot assume that his client possesses

a full fund of knowledge, experience, and sensitivity

of the qualities needed to appreciate a work.

I was once helped considerably in my desire to

better understand the work of an abstract artist who

took the trouble to show me some of the preparatory

sketches which he had employed in developing a

moving, but very complex, abstract work. As I

examined these preparatory drawings, I gained enough

insight into the artist's point of departure to give

me a grasp of the special symbolic language which

this artist had developed as part of his esthetic

idiom. It was all the aid I needed and it involved

me deeply in the artist's work. His interests now

became my interests. I acquired the work.

As the prospective client views the works, the

artist should try to engage him in discussion, not

simply regarding the merits of the artist's work, but,

more directly, regarding those relative values which

could lead to his discriminating choice -- to his acquiring one or more of these particular works. For example, one might ask the client which of the first three works he has seen he likes best. Also, ask him to indicate the things he most dislikes about these works or which of the three works he likes least, and why. In this way, one can discover a good deal about the prospect's esthetic interests, his preferences, his biases. It might even be possible to show the client something about his own viewpoint which he previously did not fully comprehend.

It is always counter-productive to assume that the collector's interests and views are precisely congruent with those of the artist. The prospect is a developing individual. He needs to learn to express his views and to understand his preferences. The artist who helps him to do this may find that he has made contact with a personality worthy of his attention and respect. The collector is defining for himself what he wants from art as well as from this artist. This is the primary clue to the artist-salesman which determines the objective possibility of making a sale.

When a client indicates that he does not appreciate a work because he does not "understand" it, do not hesitate to point out that many fine works are not fully comprehended at first sight even by the most experienced collectors. The language of many contemporary artists is difficult. It may take considerable effort to master, but those collectors who take the trouble are generally very happy that they did. As a collector studies a group of works, his involvement with them is likely to increase.

Although much has been written in recent years about the power of visual materials to instantaneously involve and move people in a non-verbal way, one cannot accomplish anything with a work of art until he takes the trouble to look carefully at it, to react to it, to reflect on it. Lasting reactions are seldom really instantaneous and subliminal. More often, they require concentration, comparison, even discussion.

To go one step further, the artist might lead the collector's attention in any of a number of valid esthetic directions by focusing him on color, form, surface, emotion, reference, subject, or object, where it is appropriate. When the collector begins to grapple with a discussion of the symbols he finds in a work or when he identifies his emotional responses to a surface, his interest and his appreciation are likely to improve because his attention has been directed into a meaningful channel.

As the encounter between artist and collector proceeds, the artist should remember that the prospect's experience with this finished work is necessarily quite different from the artist's experience which probably reached its own zenith _during_ the creative process -- not afterwards. The collector may be moved by something which was moving to the artist long ago or by something which has only interested the artist rather incidentally. But, the work of art has now acquired a life of its own. Its ability to amuse -- or amaze -- the viewer may not specifically coincide with the artist's recollected intentions.

The Trial Close

By now, the artist-salesman should be ready to move to the next step in the selling process. Presuming that the client has expressed greater preference of interest in certain works as compared with others he has seen, the artist may initiate a "trial close." A trial close question may be any of a series of questions about the client's reaction to the work, which may be answered either positively or negatively at an appropriate point in the sales presentation.

The artist might ask whether the collector likes this particular work as much as he likes a particular work he already owns. He might ask whether the work being examined seems to have certain qualities of color, form, substance, or reference which the collector finds provocative or interesting. Essentially, he wants to know if the presentation is succeeding.

If the answer to the trial close question is negative, the salesman has created an opportunity to learn something about the collector's buying problems. The prospect may have a difficulty, a point of confusion, or an objection which stands in the way of completing the sale. If this problem can be identified and resolved, the chances of selling the work will be greatly improved.

For example, if the prospect has picked one work as more exciting to him than three others he has seen, the artist might ask whether he can "visualize this work on the wall of his living room." If the collector answers affirmatively, the artist may move directly to a discussion of how the work might be framed or whether he would like to write a check for the price of the work.

If the client answers negatively, then the matter must be pursued further. What prevents the customer from visualizing the work on his wall? Perhaps he feels it is very interesting but "out of scale" for his living room. Perhaps he thinks the dominant colors of the work might be discordant with the decor of the room's furnishings. The explanation of his negative answer will tell the artist-salesman a great deal about where the client stands with regard to buying this -- or, indeed any other -- work.

In some cases, it will be possible to resolve the client's objections by showing him that the colors do <u>not</u> clash with his decor or that the scale of the work is indeed quite appropriate to the room size. In other cases, the artist may elect to show certain works which come closer to solving the client's space or color limitations.

Shortly, we will consider a series of commonly-repeated objections, together with alternative responses. One of these replies will be logical and appropriate to the specific circumstances of any client's problem. Actually, the collector, in discussing his difficulties openly with the artist-salesman is also developing his own specifications regarding what he wants and why he wants it. An intelligent purchase decision can be made only when the prospect and the artist-salesman both clearly understand the customer's needs and preferences and when these requirements can in fact be either modified or met by the artist's work.

It does nobody any particular service if the client comes away saying the familiar litany, "I don't know anything about art...but, I know what I like." An intelligent collector will want to know at least a little about the art he has been studying and a good deal more about what he likes and why he likes it. The artist-salesman should help the collector to answer these questions, in terms of his own work.

The Question of Price

Up to this point, price has not been introduced into the discussion at all. The exact price of a work of art should not be a <u>primary</u> consideration, even with a client of limited means. After all, the easiest way for the client to "save" money is to not buy <u>any</u> art at all. This is true of all discretionary purchases. Once the "necessaries" of life have been provided, it is possible for a customer to consider the really important things in life... purchases which are <u>necessary</u>, in an entirely different sense. We "need" art not for economic but for cultural reasons.

The very fact that the collector is present
in your studio -- considering the purchase of an
art work -- indicates that the collector is prepared
to acquire something beyond the common requirements
of life -- for the purpose of enhancing the
environment in which he lives and works. Economic
considerations may be important, but they should be
secondary in such a situation.

When a client raises the question of price too
early in a private sales presentation, he may be
signalling his fear that he is "over his head."
Try not to reply with a specific price, but offer
him general price categories. For example, you might
indicate that the works which you are planning to
show him range in price from $250 up through $1,500,
depending upon the size, complexity, and esthetic
significance of the work.

But suggest that it would be best to defer the
question of a specific price until the client has
selected those works which interest him most.

You might wish to go on to ask whether the "range" of prices of your works is too wide. The artist could offer not to show those works where the price is beyond the prospect's price limits at this time. Another section of this text deals at length with the problems of establishing prices for art works.

The most important thing to remember about the price of an art work is that it is not the most important thing about that work, from anyone's viewpoint. Discussing specific prices, in the abstract -- independent of a client's genuine interest and involvement in a particular work -- is a misleading line of conversation. Try first to stimulate interest, appreciation, and a desire to acquire a specific work.

A discussion of prices becomes meaningful after the client's commitment to a work has been rather clearly indicated. If a client is sincerely moved by a particular work which happens to be a little more expensive than another work which evokes no interest, the difference in price is really a

trivial matter. Such works should not be competing
with each other in terms of their relative price,
but only in terms of their relative esthetic interest
for the collector.

Once the prospect has shown a positive involvement in a work, and as part of the next step, it is
appropriate to discuss price. At that point, the
discussion is no longer dealing abstractly with prices.
The artist should freely and confidently quote the
price of a work which the prospect is actively
thinking about buying because it is an appropriate
thing to do. Too often, a misplaced emphasis on
the prices of the works being studied produces a
counter-productive situation and a misplaced focus.

Handling Objections Commonly Raised by Art Buyers - Alternate Approaches

Art works vary widely in medium, quality, size,
and image. The reactions which they provoke in
individual collectors differ greatly. But, the
objections which are raised by collectors to the

purchase of works are remarkably few in number.
They may be categorized easily and alternative
methods of handling them may be developed in
advance. These methods will work best when an
artist-salesman has thought them through carefully
and really believes himself to be correct.

Before the artist can begin to consider the
appropriate response to a client's objection, he
should determine its legitimacy and its importance.
If a prospective client has been previously qualified
before he views the work; if, that is, he has
stated that he is genuinely interested in building
a collection, acquiring a particular artist's work,
or adding works representative of a specific school
or variety of images to his collection, then his
objections may well be real and significant.

On the other hand, even some qualified prospective
buyers, when they find themselves in an uncomfortable
situation, are unwilling to embarrass themselves or
the artist by telling the truth. Rather than admit
that the works which he is viewing simply arouse no

interest or are too expensive, a collector may
fall back to a false objection with which he is
more at ease. In this case, he may hide his real
objection behind a false facade.

The artist-salesman is faced with a dilemma
whenever the collector raises an objection. He
must determine whether this objection is legitimate
and significant. Suppose, for example, the
collector has said that he thinks the work is
"too large" for his living room wall. The seller
must decide whether this is a serious objection or
perhaps just a cover-up for a larger problem. Again,
the client's remark could be just a passing comment
not requiring any attention at all. How is the
artist to judge the reality and the importance of
the collector's objection?

A highly-skilled salesman can often judge
intuitively whether the objections being made by the
collector are genuine and significant or bogus and
unimportant to the collector himself. Lacking a
fine-tuned intuition, the artist-salesman must test

the buyer. For example, in the case described here, he might say, "suppose that I can resolve this problem -- that the work seems too big for you. Is the work otherwise interesting enough that you would want to have it in your possession permanently?" Alternatively, he might say, "I think that I just might be able to show you works with comparable qualities which are somewhat smaller in scale. Do you believe that such works would be more attractive candidates for your collection?"

In each case, the artist is bringing the argument right back to a discussion of the collector's fundamental esthetic interests. If the interest is not actually there, then any proposed solution to the stated objection is trivial. But, if the collector fundamentally likes the image and can offer no additional objections, a solution to this problem will usually lead to a sale. A good salesman welcomes a chance to discuss legitimate problems with his client -- because it is a sure route to sales.

Any customer's objections may be dealt with in
only a few ways. First, the salesman may
substantially ignore the objection if he feels
that it is trivial to the client. Thus, many
customers feel obliged to grouse about prices
whenever they get the opportunity. We all complain
about inflation. This does not always mean anything significant. The artist may be well advised
to ignore or treat lightly a complaint regarding a
quoted price.

Second, the collector may be voicing a problem
which can be best resolved if the artist expresses
himself more fully. If he decides that his meaning
has not been fully grasped, the artist can go more
deeply into his position -- discussing his
symbolism or his theory of color in greater detail.
Sometimes, a good treatment of the artist's position
can clear up a difficulty for the client.

In other cases, the artist may elect to resolve
the client's problem by accomodating to it. He may

show a smaller work, a more representational image,
a less flamboyant combination of colors. Not
every effort to accomodate to the needs of the
client should be viewed as a "sell-out." Truth-to-tell,
the artist himself may once have had needs or limitations
quite similar to those of the collector. It may be
that the accomodation will open an avenue of development for the client which is not otherwise available.

Finally, in still other instances, the artist
may attempt to overcome the collector's objections
by showing that they are not valid. The artist is,
after all, probably the greatest living authority
on his own work. He knows a good deal about color,
scale, esthetic values, etc. -- in the most
professional sense. Therefore, his views should
carry great weight with the collector, if he
expresses them clearly and with confidence.

These, then, are the artist-salesman's four
alternative approaches. They may be applied to just
about any objection. The artist may _ignore_, _explain_,
accomodate, or _overcome_. The best approach will
depend upon the circumstances.

Handling Objections - Different Classes of Problems

One of the most commonly encountered client
objections might be called the "esthetic confusion"
problem. Here, the prospect is interested in and
attracted to the work, but cannot convince himself
that his attraction is deep enough or "real."
If we can determine that the objection is legitimate --
the collector has no other underlying objections --
then the alternate lines of resolution are clear.

Our task is one of showing that while the work
may seem unfamiliar, enigmatic, even strange, as it
becomes more familiar to the viewer, his interest
will grow and his appreciation will deepen. One
artist might describe comparable experiences of
other collectors with his works from the same period
to demonstrate this point. This is a good use of
testimonials. Another might relate his own developing
reactions to this particular work. In either instance,
the point is that the collector's appreciation of
the work will improve, like good wine, with age.

In these approaches, the artist is arguing that
the objection will be overcome as the work grows
more familiar. The artist might, alternatively,
accomodate to the objection simply by offering
another work which he hopes will not prove as
confusing, esthetically. Which approach will work
best depends on the nature of the work and the needs
of the collector.

A variant of the esthetic confusion problem is
one in which the prospective buyer indicates that he
thinks he likes the work, but really "does not
understand it." Here the collector may be expressing
his insecurity with regard to his own taste. Many
collectors -- even some who have been buying art works
for many years -- are insecure about the quality of
their taste. When a client says that he does not
"understand" a work, it does not necessarily follow
that he does not like it or that he is unwilling to
buy it. A good response to this objection involves
asking the client to try to indicate what he <u>does</u>
understand about the work.

This approach will involve the client more
deeply in a study of the work and give the artist
an opportunity to guide or encourage the buyer to
a better sense of security with regard to his own
appreciation of it. Occasionally, where the artist
is familiar with the client's collection, he may
use this knowledge as an aid in handling this type
of objection. For example, he might say, "did
you fully understand so-and-so's work when you first
acquired it?" or "hasn't your appreciation of
such-and-such a work deepened since you made it part
of your collection?" Here, the artist is trying to
get the collector to "explain" the problem away --
to their mutual satisfaction.

Still another objection commonly raised by
prospective collectors might be called "the socio-
logical insecurity" problem. The prospect may say,
"I like this work very much, but I am afraid that
my friends will think me foolish, if I hang it in
my home." One logical approach to this objection --
again providing that the collector's comment proves

to be legitimate -- would be to indicate that collectors of good contemporary art works are generally considered peculiar only by those of their friends who understand less about art than they do. However, the artist might add, the collector's more sophisticated acquaintances will recognize the value of the work under discussion and others will follow, in time.

An artist I know once answered this type of objection by indicating that he fully expected the collector's friends to follow him in collecting the artist's work, as soon as their appreciation ripened. Here the objection was turned into an advantage. The collector was being asked to identify himself as a taste-maker and a cultural leader, rather than an eccentric. The artist disagreed with the viewpoint expressed by the client and attempted to overcome it by showing why it was wrong-headed.

Sometimes collectors are unfamiliar with the prices currently demanded by artists of a given calibre and reputation for works of a given size and quality. They may demonstrate this lack of information by expressing concern that the work is over-priced. As suggested earlier, this objection should not be treated seriously unless the client has clearly indicated that it is a _real_ problem. That is, if the price were "right," the client would like to acquire the work. Many good sales are lost, because the artist "caves in" on the price question before first testing the legitimacy of the collector's objection.

Instead of enhancing the collector's regard for a work, an eagerness to discount or otherwise reduce prices can have the effect of convincing the collector that the work is really not worth too much in the first place. To overcome the objection of a collector who is legitimately concerned that a work may be improperly priced, the artist can indicate that he regularly gets this price and more for works of comparable size and quality. He might also suggest that his own study of the recent sales of the works of other artists with comparable reputations indicates that this work is, in fact, quite fairly priced.

In some cases, the artist may be able to state honestly that his prices have been gradually rising over a period of time and that he has reason to believe that his own works of comparable size and quality will appreciate even more over the next few years, as he becomes better known. From this point of view, the price may turn out to be quite reasonable. Such a reply has serious ramifications which are discussed later in this text. It should only be used if it is actually true, and then with some caution, as it may permanently prejudice the collector against this artist if it turns out that his prices have not been rising significantly. Again, in this case, the artist is attempting to overcome the collector's objections.

Another objection, closely related to the overpricing problem is the "cheating/swindling" problem. Everyone is aware that unscrupulous artists and art dealers have misrepresented and otherwise defrauded collectors from time to time. The prospective buyer may indicate that he is worried about the physical stability of the work which he is thinking of buying. He may be afraid that he is being short-changed in some other way.

The best reply an artist can make to this concern -- if the objection is not simply a cover-up for a more real problem -- is that he intends to remain active in the art world for the rest of his life. The artist should point out that he can ill-afford to produce shoddy work or to misrepresent the relative value of his works. The collector should be made to appreciate that the artist's professional reputation for integrity is just as important to him as if he were a doctor or an attorney.

The artist might also point out that he
hopes to enjoy a long and happy business relationship with the collector, which would be impossible
if the collector were mistreated in any way. It is,
of course, impossible and improper for anyone to
wear his integrity pinned to his chest, but an
artist must guard and cultivate his reputation for
honesty and ethical business practices carefully.
In a world where so much cheating occurs, he should
not be surprised to encounter wary clients -- he
should be happy to explain his position on this issue
patiently and tolerantly.

Another commonly raised objection finds the
house-proud collector worrying about clashing colors,
conflicting styles, and "overwhelming" objects.
The artist may be displeased to learn that a
collector is unwilling to accept a work because its
colors clash with those employed by some decorator
in the client's living room. He could try to
overcome this problem, indicating that most art
collectors recognize that the colors of the work

of art need not stand in absolute harmony to the decor of a home. Or he may explain his position by showing that the colors of his work are really compatible with those in the collector's home.

He might also suggest that the decor of a modern home is rather transitory and more apt to pall on its occupants than the color values of a fine work of art. In any case, the artist's authority, as one who works with color and form professionally, should be asserted and employed to help resolve the problem. A decor objection may be explained away or it may be overcome.

Probably the most difficult objection for the artist arises from the collector who is naturally weak-willed or dilatory in his decision-making habits. He may indicate that he wants to "think over" what he has seen or that he does not want to move "too fast." Since the artist cannot readily change the personality of the buyer, he may have to accomodate himself to such objections by agreeing to wait while the collector thinks things over or "looks around."

It would be wise, however, if before leaving the private sales presentation without a sale, the artist at least narrows down the collector's field of choice. He might ask, for example, "If you were to select one work from all you have seen this evening, which would it be?" or "From which two would you make your selection, and why?"

In some cases, the artist may elect to encourage the dilatory buyer to take a few works home with him so that he can see how they "work." This is generally a dangerous procedure -- especially with a new client -- since the artist cannot be sure of the integrity of the prospective buyer or even of his ability to properly care for the works he takes home. Further, the artist's insurance coverage is probably void when the work is removed from its normal storage place.

When the collector asks to take home a work on trial, the artist might reply, "Yes, you may take this work home on the basis of a thirty-day free exchange privilege. I'll need a one-third deposit, of course." Thus, the work is not being "loaned."

It is actually being purchased -- with the provision

that it may be exchanged within a month if the

prospective client decides that he prefers a

different work. Now, the client is being asked

to match the artist's desire for a sale by

indicating his own seriousness of purpose.

The foregoing discussion shows a variety of

common objections and possible approaches to

handling each of them, presuming that they are

legitimate. The reader may wish to employ the

appended check-list to review these objections.

In each case, the collector's problem is either

explained, accomodated, or overcome. On the other

hand, the approaches suggested are not the only

ones which could have been utilized. An alternative

approach might have actually been more appropriate

in a particular instance.

Finally, the novice salesman must learn that not all qualified prospects will buy -- no matter how well the salesman handles his client. To be sure, he should be prepared for a variety of objections, and he should try to learn to distinguish a real problem from a contrived excuse. He should also appreciate that not all collectors will buy his works. He only needs a fair share of the market and this is accessible if he handles his collectors with reasonable care.

Handling Objections Which Collectors
Commonly Raise to Buying Works of Art

Objection	Customer's Catch-phrases	Alternative Approaches Ignore,* Explain, Accomodate, Overcome
1. Esthetic confusion.	"I'm not sure I like it." "I'm not sure why I'm attracted to it."	a) "Others did not appreciate it at first, but now they do." b) "This work will grow more meaningful in time."
2. Esthetic confusion (Variant)	"I'm not sure I understand it."	a) "What is it that you do understand about it?" b) "Your understanding will improve in time."
3. Sociological Insecurity.	"I like it, but I'm afraid my friends will think me foolish."	a) "Your most knowledgeable friends will love it." b) "Let others follow you."
4. Economic Insecurity.	"That price seems rather high."	a) "It is not high for a work of this quality." b) "Actually, this price may prove to be very reasonable in the long view."**
5. The Scoundrel Syndrome.	"How do I know I'm not being cheated or fooled?"	a) "My integrity as a professional artist is your best warranty."
6. The Decor Problem.	"The colors will clash." "The scale is too large for my home."	a) "Colors need not harmonize." b) "Try a smaller work." c) "Art is long. Decor is brief."
7. Dilatory Behavior.	"I simply cannot make up my mind today."	a) "But, which works do you like best at this time?" b) "What do you like most about these works?"

*One possible reply, if an objection seems trivial, unreal, or a "cover-up", is to avoid answering it.
**Use only when almost certainly true, and then with caution.

118.

Closing the Sale

Once the client's real objections have been explained away, accomodated, or overcome, and he has responded agreeably to a new trial close question, the artist-salesman is ready to move to the final step in the selling process. This is known as "the close." Closing a sale is sometimes considered the most difficult task in selling because it involves a certain finesse which can only be acquired after some practice. But closing, like everything else related to selling, can be learned by anyone who wants to acquire the skill.

The artist-salesman should never attempt to close a sale until he is certain that the client has an expressed or implied interest in the possibility of owning one or more of the works which he has been examining. Premature closing efforts can confuse and offend the client. They are a mark of the novice salesman's insensitivity to the level of interest of his prospective collector. When a positive reaction has been indicated and the client's desires are clear, as indicated by his responses, the artist may employ

any of a number of standard closing techniques to

assist a hesitant buyer.

For instance, if the client is unable to decide

between two works which he feels he likes equally

well, the artist might suggest -- with some authority --

that he would be happy to arrange for the client to

acquire both works since they are complementary and

will enhance his collection as a pair. Or, the

artist might suggest, on the basis of prior

discussion, that one of the two works is the best

one for the client, at this time, and that the

other might still be acquired at a later date.

In either case, the salesman is helping the

client to better define or narrow his field of

choice, a task which should be much easier for

the artist than it is for the collector, who may

be viewing the works for the first time. A

failure to decide on a particular choice can result

in the collector leaving the presentation having

made no choice at all. This is most unfortunate. For all their good intentions, only a handful of collectors will be able to recollect the works well enough to sort out their feelings once they have left the private sales presentation.

Related to the choice-narrowing close is the "assumed sale" close -- probably the most widely used of all closing techniques. Here the artist-salesman, recognizing the genuine, if hesitant, interest of the collector, simply assumes that a sale has been made. He promptly moves on to questions of delivery, framing, method of payment, etc. The collector quickly recognizes this ploy. He may restrain the artist without difficulty if he chooses to do so or simply allow him to proceed.

To help him with this approach, the artist-salesman may pick up his sales invoice form and carefully complete it, noting the customer's name and address, the date, description and dimensions of the work, the price, method of delivery, etc.

He should then offer the form to the collector to
check and initial. Few collectors will be
offended if this approach is employed gracefully
and intelligently. It simply formalizes and
finalizes a business transaction that was clearly
being consummated anyhow.

There are a number of other closing techniques
which may be utilized when they are appropriate.
One widely used method of closing the sale of an
art work is the "time-value" technique. Here an
artist may point out that the work under consideration
is indeed one of his best works still available.
But, it can be expected to be off the market in a
short time because it is so desirable. As every
merchant and attorney knows, time is the essence of
most business activities.

The client, in this case, is urged to make a
positive decision before his purchase opportunity
is lost. This closing device is particularly
appropriate where the artist's market is, in fact,
fairly active. As in other cases, it is a reckless
salesman who misrepresents the actual circumstances

of the case. He could be embarrassed many
months later to have to admit that the work is
still available.

A more consistently valid variant of the
time-value close involves a recognition that
certain kinds of purchasing opportunities have
a way of not recurring. Thus, the artist might
point out that it may be some time before the
collector will be able to get together with the
artist again. He might add -- if it is true --
that the work will be offered to another collector
shortly, if it is not sold on the present occasion.

I know a major contemporary art dealer who
employs the time-value close with great success
when he is visiting cities distant from his home base.
In this case, the collector indeed, has a limited
time available to view and buy this dealer's works
because the dealer is expecting to return to his home
city shortly. He tells me that he generally gets a
faster and better response from a qualified prospect
in a distant city, because he employs this approach,

which he cannot use with his regular home-based
clients.

Still another commonly-used closing technique
is the negotiated or "fairy god-mother" close,
where the artist helps an uncertain or undecided
client to reach a conclusion by granting a "boon"
of some sort. For example, the artist may say,
"if it will encourage you, I am willing to supervise
the framing of this work, and I will help you hang it
in your home so that you can be assured it will
make the best impression and be ready for the
reception you are planning."

Or he might say, "To help you to reach a
decision, I will sell you all three of the works
which you like best. But, instead of requiring full
cash payment, which is my usual custom, I will take
one-third down and the balance within ninety days,
at no additional charge." Such negotiated concessions
or "boons" sometimes give the collector a significant
added impetus in the direction of making a positive

purchase decision at the time of the private sales
presentation. A boon which should not be offered
is an unearned discount as this impairs the artist's
pricing structure. This issue is discussed more
fully in the section on pricing.

As suggested earlier, many art dealers, and a
few artists commonly employ a closing technique
which might be called the "investment appreciation"
close. They indicate -- as an inducement, and often
without foundation -- that the works under consideration
are likely to appreciate considerably in market value,
within a short time.

Statements of this kind can actually harm the
long-term interests of the artist if they turn out
to be false. Certainly, some art works have
appreciated significantly in market value -- sometimes
because of a prodigious growth in interest for the
artist's work and sometimes due to intense and
artificial promotion. Also, some works were under-
priced to begin with. But not every artist's works
will appreciate significantly in value. The whole
idea has been wildly exaggerated.

When a collector has asked a relatively unknown

artist about the possible appreciation of his

investment, he might honestly reply in this way:

> Sir, investments vary in terms of their
> appreciation potential. Blue chip
> stocks may be high in cost and slow to
> appreciate, but they pay dividends
> regularly. Growth stocks are
> relatively expensive, measured in terms
> of earnings, but they may have a
> reassuring growth history to justify
> their price. My work as a relatively
> unknown artist might be compared to
> a new stock issue.
>
> It may indeed improve in value over
> the years. I hope it will. On the
> other hand, this is a gamble because
> the market price of the work may not
> change at all or might even deteriorate.
> Since I am not well-known, my works
> are rather reasonably priced. If you
> like them well enough to own them,
> then they are indeed a bargain, quite
> aside from any possible investment
> appreciation. My best collectors do
> not plan to sell my works or donate
> them to institutions to reap a tax
> benefit. Please think of the
> appreciation potential as a risk which
> might pay significant returns, but
> which is strictly a secondary reason
> for buying my work.

This approach brings the closing argument back

where it belongs, to the context of the intrinsic

esthetic merits of the work and the interest which the work provokes in the collector. The best closing argument -- and the best reason for buying any work -- is its esthetic interest, the excitement it suggests or the impact which it can generate on the collector's psyche or on his environment.

As the client becomes more personally involved in an artist's work, his opportunity to appreciate this grows. The artist-salesman's job is one of helping him to follow the logic of his own convictions. In the last analysis, the only valid reason for buying an art work is its merit, as recognized by the collector. Without interest, any collector's acquisitions are built on sand.

Contrary to the popular view of the collector as one who has little concern other than the crass need for prestige, the good opinion of his friends, or the economic appreciation of his collection, every real art collector realizes -- even if only subconsciously -- that what counts most is the quality of his selections from an esthetic view-point. If his prestige grows, it may be because his taste is good. If the works increase in value, perhaps -- here too -- it is because the collector has selected good works.

Commonly Used Closing Methods

Method	Artist-Salesman's Key-phrase
1. Choice-Narrowing Close	"As I see it, you really seem to prefer this work to all the others."
2. Assumed Sale Close	"I think you are making a very wise choice. May I deliver this work to your home on Monday?"
3. Time-Value Close	"Better buy now, while this desirable work is still available." "We have been so long getting together, I fear that further delay will cost you the opportunity to own this fine work."
4. Negotiated Close – The Fairy God-Mother's Boon	"To solve the dilemma, why not take both works? I'll help by waiting 90 days for final payment."
5. Investment Appreciation Close	"This work may well improve in value." (N.B. Such an assertion can be harmful if it proves untrue.)
6. Esthetic Appreciation Close	"Buy this work because, if you do, it will still be stimulating long afterward."

Recording the Sales Transaction

Once a sale has been made, a sales invoice should be prepared. Multi-part form books for this purpose may be purchased in most stationery stores. Many small businessmen prefer to prepare their own invoice forms. A sample is appended. It should be pre-numbered and used consecutively so that every form may be audited and accounted for. The invoice should be prepared in duplicate, with one copy retained by the artist and the other going to the collector with the work. An art dealer should prepare his invoices in triplicate, keeping one copy for himself, another for the client, and a third for the artist.

The form should show the date of sale, the name and address of the client, the name of the artist, and a description of the works sold, including title, dimensions, medium, and date of execution. The price for the work, cash or volume discount, if any, sales tax, if applicable, freight

John Doe, Artist
1234 W. First Street
Middletown, Ohio 23456   Telephone: (312) 435-9222

No. 12345

SALES INVOICE

Terms				BankAmericard	☐		
Net		Cash Sale	☐	Master Charge	☐	C.C. #	

Ship		Bill		Date
to:		to:		Via

Item No.	Description: Medium, Title, Dimensions (Ht. X Width)	Price

All sales subject to terms and conditions on reverse of this invoice.

Received in good condition:	Net	$
	Sales Tax	$
Client's Signature Date	Total	$

Terms and Conditions of Sale

Payment for all works herein shall be in
United States currency, net, on presentation of
this invoice. Works may also be charged on valid
Bankamericard/Mastercharge credit accounts.

Unless otherwise specifically indicated, all
works herein are originals, executed by the artist
and are certified to be free from all defects due
to faulty craftsmanship or faulty materials for a
period of twelve months from the date of sale.
If flaws should occur during this period and
appear to be due to these causes, said works
shall be subject to repair or replacement, at the
option of the Seller. Buyer is cautioned, however,
that the Seller cannot be responsible for fading,
cracking, and other damage to these works caused
by improvident exposure to sunlight and weather.

The Buyer may return any work acquired herein
for full credit against the purchase of any other
works available at that time, provided only that
said work shall be returned in good condition
and within 30 days from the date herein.

All shipments are fully insured by the
Seller against damage or loss. If works are not
received in good condition please notify the
Seller at once.

All shipments are F.O.B. the artist's studio
and will be transferred via freight collect,
unless prepaid by the Buyer. Crating methods
and charges are per art object freight company
standard procedures and rates.

and insurance liability, and the down payment and balance due, if any, should also be shown. On the back of the customer's copy of the custom printed sales invoice form, it is wise to print the artist's terms and conditions of sale. The sample form shown here has been adapted by a number of artists and art dealers.

It may be a good idea to ask the client to sign your copy of the invoice to indicate that he has received the work in good condition. It is also wise to get a signature when some money is still outstanding on the purchase.

This sales record will be useful for many purposes, including income tax and sales tax preparation and collection of outstanding balances due. The most important function of the invoice is that it tells you what you have sold, to whom, when, and at what price and terms. Such records will be very important to your future marketing efforts. They should be filed in a safe place.

Cultivating Clients for Repeat Business

Well-established artists find that much of their new work is sold to collectors who already own one or more of their earlier works. If an artist has a good deal to say in his work, or a variety of interpretations of a certain image, he is probably worthy of being collected "in depth." The artist should try to cultivate a number of collectors who are interested in developing a broadly representative collection of his various periods and modes of expression. This is his "following" and constitutes a most important aspect of his career.

Once a collector has acquired a work by the artist, he should be elevated to a special status in that artist's future marketing efforts. His index card should be removed from the Contact File and placed in a Client's File. He should not only receive a Christmas card annually, but should also be invited to studio parties, exhibition openings, lecture-demonstrations, and any other special events which might interest him further in the artist's career and future output.

In some cases, the artist may wish to encourage his best collectors to lend works for special museum exhibitions or to illustrate art magazine articles. In others, he may encourage his collectors to bring their friends to his studio for simple activities such as a Sunday morning brunch or a special studio exhibition and sale. The artist's collectors should come to feel that they are important to the artist -- as indeed they are.

Old, established customers are always the best source of new business, either in terms of their own needs or as expressed in the interests of their friends. Developing such clients out of more casual buyers is a time-consuming but, ultimately, a very rewarding task. To be sure, some collectors abuse their priveleges and make extraordinary demands on the artist's time. Care should be taken to avoid this level of entanglement.

But, the artist's economic security depends,
in most cases, directly on his collectors' continuing
and deepening interest in his career. Occasionally,
a collector will lose interest in an artist's
image as it develops, or he will find it
economically necessary to suspend his acquisition
activity. In most cases, he should not be discarded,
His interest may return and his economic capacities
may be revived. Just about every former client is
a prospect for further sales if proper follow-up
is maintained.

Steps to Follow in Selling Art
Through Private Sales Presentations

Step:

Artist-Salesman's Key-phrase:

A. Locate and qualify the prospect.*

"I think I'll be able to show you that some of my works belong in your collection."

B. Formally present selected works under restricted viewing conditions.**

"Why do you like this work better than the other?"

C. Heighten interest in the works shown

"Tell me what you find in this area of the work."

D. Attempt a trial close.

"Can you see how this work might enhance your collection?"

E. Identify and answer valid objections

"I believe that your appreciation of this work will deepen as you live with it."

F. Close the sale

"May I help you select the framing for this work?"

G. Prepare a sales invoice

"Will you please initial this invoice, here?"

H. Follow-up on your client. Old customers are your most reliable supporters.

"When I finished these new works, I thought of you at once."

---

*Well-established artists will already have a number of collectors, some of whom are a regular source of repeat sales and referrals. Even so, they should always be interested in locating and developing new prospective collectors.

**It is possible to sell works under less formal circumstances, but this method is much more likely to succeed.

Conducting a Weekend Studio Exhibition

The traditions of the art market in the United States are such that "clearance sales" are almost unknown and certainly frowned upon. To most collectors, they carry a connotation of cheap commercialism -- and perhaps even of desperation -- ill-suited to the marketing of art works. Accordingly, active art dealers and successful artists do not conduct sales, as such, but rather employ the technique of the "exhibition" -- a one-man or group show -- to stimulate floor traffic and to widen the seller's marketing contacts.

Emulating this activity, in addition to seeking private sales presentation opportunities, the artist who sells his own work might well consider conducting an exhibition in his own studio over a weekend or on two consecutive weekends. Such an exhibition has all the positive ramifications of a sale, without any of the negative connotations implied by such terms as "markdown," "clearance," or "bargain." Works shown at an exhibition are indeed generally available for sale, but they are not distressed merchandise

or factory close-outs, and they should never be so treated.

It seems reasonable then that no price tags should be attached to the works or mounted near them. Studio exhibitions should not be over-stocked, nor should works be badly hung or poorly illuminated. Graphics should not be treated disrespectfully as some artists and dealers do when they place them in a "dump" bin -- without protection -- for un-attended browsing, as though they were potatoes or day-old bakery products.

Planning a successful studio exhibition may require the preparation of a mailing list which is larger than the artist's own list. An artist can enlarge his mailing list by trading lists with other artists. Others employ the roster of a local museum association or the rosters of other community cultural institutions such as the local symphony society's patron list.

As indicated earlier, direct mail advertising companies will prepare mailing lists of individuals with specific professional, residence, or income characteristics. For example, it may be possible to compile a mailing list of all those dentists, doctors, and lawyers residing in certain postal zones relatively close to the artist's studio.

The proper size of a mailing list is a matter of experimentation. Generally, if the artist is seeking two or three hundred viewers over a weekend, he might decide to mail out four to six thousand invitations, on the premise that one recipient in twenty will respond. With a better list the response rate might be higher.

While the mailing list is being developed, the artist should prepare a mailing piece or brochure, announcing his forthcoming studio exhibition. This announcement need not be expensive, but it should be legible, attractive, and informative. The information included on the brochure should indicate that a studio exhibition is to take place on certain dates, between certain hours.

The name of the artist and a few brief
biographical references or a pithy critical
comment should be given, together with the address
of the studio. If the location is hard to find,
a simple map might be included. A more elaborate
announcement might also include an illustration of
one or more of the works or a picture of the artist
at work in his studio. When a work is shown and
the illustration does not indicate its scale
visually, the dimensions should be given.

These announcements should be mailed via first
class, hand-stamped mail, timed to arrive about ten
days before the first day of the exhibition. If
they are sent earlier, attendance can be impaired
because potential clients may misplace an announcement
if it has been around the house too many days. If
it is sent as bulk mail, the announcement may not
be read at all -- or may arrive too late.

A press release and a high-contrast, glossy
photo should be sent to the local or community press

timed to arrive about two weeks before the studio
exhibition opening. Many local papers will carry
such a release. So too, the neighborhood editions
of the metropolitan papers should receive this
material. The art pages of the larger papers
seldom notice such events, unless the artist is
rather well established.

As the guests arrive at the artist's studio,
they should be encouraged by the artist's spouse or
friend to sign a guest book, recording their names,
addresses and phone numbers. The works shown at
such an exhibition should be simply framed or matted
and hung with particular care for proper lighting.
Works should not be allowed to rest casually on tables,
chairs or floors, since they might easily be damaged
or destroyed unless they are in some way "set up" for
exhibition. Three-dimensional objects must be fixed
securely on pedestal stands or on tables, where it is
appropriate. Work-in-progress and other materials not
directly pertinent to the exhibition should be removed
from general view.

Generally, the grouping of works in a studio exhibition can be a little tighter than is normally appropriate for an art gallery exhibition. Even so, it is unwise to show more than forty works at one time, even in a rather large studio. Confusion can result from over-exhibiting. If a client does not see any works he likes at the exhibition, the artist may offer to have him return at another time for a private sales presentation of other works.

All the works exhibited at a studio exhibition should be numbered. A typed list of prices, referencing these numbers, should be available at the desk. Prices are usually listed for the work on an "as is" basis, that is, as displayed: framed, unframed, matted, etc.

Since a studio exhibition is a relatively informal affair, light refreshments are in order -- coffee, punch, and "finger" foods -- peanuts or potato chips. If paper napkins and plates, or plastic cups are employed, several large, covered trash receptacles should also be provided to help

keep the studio neat and reduce the probability

of spillage. A number of large ashtrays should

also be provided. Someone should be assigned the

task of regularly cleaning up after the guests, so

that the next arrivals find things neat.

In some cases, the artist may decide to show a

few works which are "not for sale" or which have

already been purchased by clients. A few round,

red, pressure-sensitive dots, indicating that certain

works already have been purchased, tend to stimulate

the interest of certain collectors. Again, it is

unwise to misrepresent the facts as this might

lead to lost sales opportunities. The artist's own

collection, which often contains a number of his best

works, should not be on display.

Care should be taken to see that the walls of

the studio are clean and well-illuminated, even if

additional decorating and lighting must be arranged

to accomplish this objective. If the works are not

attractively set and shown they will be hard to

appreciate. Our culture is -- for better or worse -- deeply committed to the concepts of good packaging and thus a carelessly mounted exhibition will detract from the reception which the works might otherwise receive.

When people arrive for the studio exhibition, they should be greeted personally and encouraged to examine the works casually, to ask questions, and to offer comments. If a couple goes through the exhibition without buying -- even without commenting -- they should be thanked for coming and encouraged to feel welcome and comfortable in the artist's studio.

The artist must remember that only a minority of his visitors will buy any works. Some will buy not at the studio exhibition but in a subsequent private sales presentation. At these, the opportunity to study and to engage the artist's work is considerably better than it is on first contact at a "stand-up" studio exhibition. But coming to the exhibition "breaks the ice" and makes a really effective presentation easier to arrange for a later date. An important function of the studio exhibition is creating just such contacts for subsequent private presentations.

Charity Sales and Auctions

In the past few decades, leaders of many charitable organizations, within the art community and outside of it, have discovered that the works of contemporary artists can be very useful for fund-raising purposes. Accordingly, many non-profit institutions regularly conduct sales of art work. Others engage in art auctions. Some sales and auctions for charitable institutions have become very significant events -- socially and economically. One such event with which I am familiar regularly produces over $100,000 per year for the sponsoring organization.

In many cases, the works sold at these fund-raising functions have been donated by the artist or by dealers and collectors to assist in financing a worthy cause -- and at the same time to enhance the artist's reputation. On some occasions, these activities may, indeed, accomplish both of these objectives. However, good intentions can sometimes go awry and cause serious damage to the artist's reputation and to his market as well.

Unfortunately, fund-raising art sales and auctions are generally conducted by well-meaning amateurs. These volunteers usually have not taken the trouble to reflect on how art should be marketed. Also, they are not deeply committed to the artists' interests but rather to the "cause" for which they are laboring. They may not even be aware that they can injure an artist's market by improperly presenting or pricing the work which has been offered for sale.

The most common abuse found at art auctions and charity sales is the "flexible" approach taken to pricing the artist's work. Since those handling the sale have no investment in the works and no real stake in the artist's future, they often feel that

<u>any</u> sum of money raised through the sale of a work is better than nothing. Thus, a work which has a market value of $750 might be sold by some well-meaning, charitable matron for $75 -- or even less -- on the . peculiar premisses that the money is all going to charity and the donor-customer is entitled to "a bargain." The same charitable lady would probably be aghast at the suggestion that her husband's business products or professional services should ever be offered at less than cost.

Such pricing practices can have a very serious negative effect on the artist's market since the buyer will undoubtedly advise his friends and associates that the works of this artist are "normally" priced within a stated range, but they are "occasionally" available to the "smart" buyer at considerably lower levels. The original price range will thus be swept aside by a new price range. Years of effort devoted to building a following which accepts a definable, steadily-rising price structure can be badly damaged by a prominent

charity auction. So too, a well-meaning collector

who donates a work to charity and claims the

allowable "fair market value" on his income tax

return may be shocked to learn that the Internal

Revenue Service representative will allow only the

depressed auction price to be deducted.

To protect his market, no artist should ever

allow a charitable institution to offer his works

for sale below a minimum price which he and his

dealer have agreed upon in advance. Professional

art auctioneers call this minimum the "reserve"

price. They understand that if this price is not

offered, the work should be either withdrawn from

the sale, or "bid-in" by an unidentified house

representative working in the audience. From the

artist's viewpoint, it is generally better to avoid

a forced sale where it might hurt the artist's

pricing structure, if the right buyer is not present.

Further, whenever a work is sold at an auction

or charity sale, the artist should insist that he be

informed regarding the buyer's name and address.
Although he may not benefit from any significant
income from such sales, he might possibly acquire
a new collector. This can be of some value to his
developing market, especially if the selling price
was firm.

The artist should also make clear to the
institution conducting the sale or the auction,
that, if the works which he donates are not sold,
they should be returned promptly, and in good
condition. Otherwise, he may be making a donation
which does not really benefit the institution he
is trying to help and his work may simply disappear
from sight. Well-meaning volunteers can be very
callous about art works which they do not own.

The patronizing view held by volunteer workers
of many charitable organizations infers that the
artist should be delighted with any small crumbs
of publicity which may be thrown his way as a result
of the charity sale or auction. Hopefully, the leaders
of organizations which engage in such sales can be

made to realize that artists and dealers who try
to help them are entitled to the same kind of respect
and consideration which would normally be given to
any other professional man who lends his time and
talent to furthering a worthy cause.

However, since there has been so much misunderstanding on this issue, I have advised my artist-
clients in recent years not to donate works for
sale or auction by charitable institutions unless
they receive a written promise from the head of
that organization assuring them:

(1) that the artist's established price will be
protected;

(2) that works for which adequate interest is
not indicated will be withdrawn in the case of sales,
and "bought-in," in the case of auctions;

(3) that the buyer's name and address will be
supplied to the artist after the sale or auction, and

(4) that unsold works will be returned in good
condition to the donor.

PRICING THE ARTIST'S WORK

Why Art Prices Have Been Rising

Unlike commodities -- which have a more utilitarian nature -- original art is not "consumed" by the buyer. Given proper care, a work of art will not wear out or lose its power to excite, please, and otherwise interest its owner. Since it possesses these unusual attributes, the work can enrich the lives of collectors in many ways and over long periods of time. An art collection often represents the best expression of the personal taste of its owners. If a collector loses interest in a work, he may find someone else to buy it or he may donate it to a museum. The growing recognition of these unusual and lasting qualities serves to buttress the price of works of art, just as it reinforces the price of diamonds and antiques.

Since the end of World War II, contemporary artists in the United States have witnessed a substantial climb in the prices which may be commanded

for their works. These increases apply not only
to the works of famous masters, but also to the
efforts of artists who are not as well-known or
as widely collected. I have discussed this
question with literally hundreds of artists.
They have all experienced significant price
increases -- if their works have any sort of market.

One reason for the sharp upward trend in art
prices is the generally inflationary character of
our economy. Money simply buys less today. Thus,
if a work of art were offered at the same price
this year as it might have brought in 1960, its
real price has declined. During the past few decades,
prices have risen in general, reflecting the inflation
with which every merchant and every consumer must
contend. In terms of the other goods and services
that money can purchase, the price of an art work
should have increased by a factor of at least
fifty percent, over the past fifteen years, just to
keep pace with inflation.

But the prices of many original art works have been climbing at a rate considerably faster than can be explained solely by inflationary factors. As the discretionary income available to the growing American middle-class has expanded, and as its members have acquired more leisure, better educations, and higher aspirations, the funds devoted to cultural pursuits have also grown. For a variety of reasons, the thirst for culture, in its many ramifications, has increased. Our art museums are generally the best-attended public facilities in every major city. Enrollment in art classes rivals or exceeds other varieties of adult education across the country. Expensive, illustrated art books enjoy substantial sales in most book stores. Business institutions seem particularly anxious to find ways of associating themselves with the works of artists as collectors, exhibitors, and sponsors.

Art dealers and artists thus find themselves in contact with thousands of new collectors -- men and women whose parents generally owned no original art.

Some of these novice collectors have only a
rudimentary acquaintance with the history of art.
Most are conscious of the need for further
development of their taste and appreciation.
But they want to own original, contemporary art
works, and they are buying -- to the best of their
ability. This increased interest exerts an upward
pressure on art prices at all levels of the market.
Even work which might in other eras have generated
little interest has a market today.

Further, the old masters of earlier generations
have been getting scarcer, entering public collections
and increasing in economic value as well. The
structure of our tax laws and their impetus on
philanthropy makes it difficult for wealthy
collectors and their heirs to retain such works
once they have appreciated significantly over their
acquisition cost. But as the major master works
enter the public domain, they disappear from the
marketplace, leaving the contemporary works to vie
for the collector's primary attention.

A careful examination of the buying habits
and motivations of different kinds of art collectors
will show that collectors seek an extension of their
own taste and experience with art when acquiring
works. In significant ways, their collecting often
parallels the creative experiences of certain
specific artists. Further, like the artist's urge
to create, the urge to collect art is self-
reinforcing and self-justifying. Thus, collectors
find the activity absorbing, exhilarating, and
important. Even for the collector of modest means,
prices are not the primary determinant of purchasing
decisions. The collector's needs and interests
determine his willingness to buy and place limits
on the price he will pay.

Elements of an Artist's Prices

The price a collector may be asked to pay for
an original work of art depends upon a number of
different -- sometimes conflicting -- factors. Some
of these factors, such as the scale of the work,

are easy to quantify. The importance of others

is a matter of judgment and experience. Their

relative significance will change, depending upon

the motivations of particular collectors and on the

shifting levels of interest to be found in our

culture.

We may divide the elements which influence the

pricing of an artist's work into three main groups:

o factors related to the intrinsic qualities
  of the work of art -- the esthetic and
  technological merits of a work,

o factors related to recovering the costs
  associated with producing and marketing
  the work, and

o factors related to extrinsic issues, such
  as the artist's reputation, the demand
  for, or the scarcity of, his work, etc.

1. Intrinsic Qualities - The Basis of Value in Art

Mr. Richard H. Rush, in his useful study,

Art As An Investment,* points out:

> Quality is the essence of art value. For a
> painting to be worth anything, it must have
> quality... a successful collector of art
> must be a person who appreciates quality in
> art. He buys because the quality is there,

---

*p. 262 ff, Prentice-Hall (1961, Englewood Cliffs, N.J.)

and he arrives at his conclusion as to the quality through his native taste, through an intense enthusiasm for art and for collecting.

For some collectors, quality in art is not an absolute as it is for others. Even so, knowledgeable collectors tell us that there are certain works within the _oeuvre_ of particular artists which have greater appeal, more significance, and deeper interest for them than other works by the same artist or by other artists with similar images or viewpoints. The fully eclectic collector who appreciates every-thing equally -- but nothing especially -- is not a major factor in the art market. He lacks the discrimination on which choice must be founded.

Whether the collector applies a set of critical standards peculiar to his own taste or shared with a number of reputable art experts has little direct effect on the price he will pay. He is in either case looking for certain qualities inherent in the work. Without these essential qualities and the interest which they provoke, there would be little demand for an artist's work. All questions regarding the recovery of production costs, the artist's reputation, and their relationship to prices, would be trivial.

Some artists imbue their work with a desirable quality simply by employing certain mechanical, structural, or manipulative techniques. The sculptor who applies an attractive patina to the surface of his work is seeking a particular visual effect through a technical process. The artist who employs motors, lights, plastics, or reflective surfaces, like the artist who employs a specialized technology, is seeking to utilize these materials, devices, and methods toward an esthetic end.

Other artists may be less concerned with objects which can be generated by such techniques and materials. They consciously avoid the use of unusual artifices. Instead, they seek to generate an esthetic experience more directly by relying primarily on their artistic ability to evoke an image which has a meaningful impact on the viewer. They use their skills in drawing, painting, designing, shaping, and abstracting to achieve this result.

In any case, the artist is striving to produce a work which has certain desirable esthetic qualities. When he succeeds, the work has value to him as an artist. Often it also has value to a collector as well. From these fundamental esthetic values, practically all of the work's economic value must ultimately be derived. Esthetic quality should form the foundation of every artist's pricing policy.

Does the work induce a pleasurable response? Is it exciting or stimulating? Is it evocative of certain emotions? Does it suggest certain significant concepts? Do the colors, lines, forms, surfaces attract the viewer, provoke him, disturb him? Is the work interesting? _Value_, as Ralph Barton Perry pointed out, _is the object of any interest_.

But the intrinsic quality of a work can refer not only to esthetic matters but also to fabrication problems and their solution. The knowledge, skill, and integrity of an artist contributes significantly to the longevity and stability of a work. An improperly stretched canvas, a poor choice of paper or ink, a careless application of plastic, or an improperly designed armature may obliterate a work's esthetic qualities in a relatively short time -- making it undesirable and unsalable.

For an artist who does not particularly concern himself with the "lasting" qualities of his work, this need not create an esthetic problem. Certainly the artist is not bound by the dictum that art is -- read "should be" -- long. But for the collector, this issue is often a significant concern. The price which an artist's works command is sure to be effected by its intrinsic structural as well as its intrinsic esthetic qualities.

Incidentally, most artists are very conscious of the fact that their esthetic success varies from work to work. Van Gogh speaks in his letters to his brother of the vast quantities of "paste" he had to generate in order to create a few "diamonds." And yet, I find many artists hesitate to express their own relative sense of achievement with differentiated prices. Often all works of comparable

size, medium, and image carry identical prices.
This suggests a puzzling unwillingness to
indicate the artist's or even his dealer's personal
preferences. When the artist makes such a judgement he can reinforce his own pricing structure
substantially.

2. Recovering Costs

A surprisingly large number of artists and
dealers are not aware of the importance of
recovering their costs from the sale of their work.
They do not seem to realize that they are otherwise
subsidizing their collectors. Many serious artists
with whom I have discussed the question have never
even bothered to calculate the actual cost of their
works. This is most unfortunate. <u>No artist or dealer</u>
<u>should ever sell art works below his cost.</u>

Of course, there may be times when an artist is
in dire straits. He may feel impelled to "sacrifice"
his work at a price which is below his actual cost.

I have been told by more than one artist that he felt he had no alternative to selling below cost. At the depth of the Depression, Arshile Gorky found it necessary to part with some of his best works at very low prices. However, jobs are relatively plentiful today, even if they are sometimes distracting or annoying. A self-respecting artist has little excuse for demeaning his own works and hurting his future market -- to say nothing of the market of other artists -- by selling his works below their cost.

There is one circumstance where this maxim about recovering the cost might be disregarded. When a young artist is trying to improve or extend his reputation by placing his works in important museum collections, he might adopt a policy which temporarily includes judicious gifts to worthy institutions. Many fine museums have miniscule acquisition budgets and simply cannot acquire all the works their directors and curators would like.

Accordingly, they depend upon gifts from generous collectors and artists for a good portion of their acquisitions.

Occasionally, an official of such an institution may abuse this practice be insisting on donations even when the museum can afford to pay for a work. By using his power as a taste-maker, the official may also insist upon unwarranted discounts. Nevertheless, an artist may find that representation in certain prestigious collections is important enough to justify what amounts to a "free sample" or a "special promotion" policy.

In my opinion, it is wiser for an artist who is trying to build his reputation to occasionally donate a work to a museum than it is for him to reduce his prices through discounting. Too often, the volunteer workers around the museum will learn of an artist's willingness to discount and will presume that they are entitled to privileges similar to those granted to the museum. Discounted prices quickly displace list prices.

Of course, the new federal tax law is discriminatory

in its treatment of the artist who donates his work

to an art museum. Where collectors may deduct market

value, the artist may deduct only a portion of his costs.

Hopefully, this law will be repealed or proven un-

constitutional. Meantime, I still believe that an

occasional promotional gift to an institution might be

warranted -- but only for a brief period in the artist's

career. In all other cases, I advise my own artist-

clients to avoid gifts and -- more particularly --

to avoid discounts unless they are warranted by the

terms discussed later in this section of the text.

Certain aspects of the cost of producing a work

of art are easily identified while others are

relatively hard to quantify. In most art media,

the cost of the primary materials employed in

making a work is rather easy to determine. Metal

costs so much per pound, a canvas of a given weight

has a certain cost per square foot. The cost of clay,

wood, and other fundamental materials employed by

artists in their work can be calculated simply and

ascribed to specific works. Sometimes the artist

buys certain materials for use exclusively on a

particular work.

However, measurable quantities of materials are

not always used on a single art work. In such cases,

their cost must be distributed over several works.

Where these materials are relatively low in cost,

their relationship to individual works need not be

too precisely determined. For example, when a sculptor

uses several boxes of welding rod in producing a number

of welded works, he may attribute such costs to the

works by roughly estimating the approximate portion

of the cost of the rods going into each work.

He may also accumulate the cost of all those

materials which cannot be directly ascribed to

individual works over a period of months. Then,

he can develop an approximate cost for all such

materials, per average hour worked or per average

work produced. This cost tends to be fairly

stable for an artist within a particular medium.

Cost estimates derived by accumulating direct material costs and then adding a factor for other incidental materials used -- based on the number of hours worked and a previously determined rate per hour -- are not precise, but they are generally adequate measures of material costs.

Labor cost is often the most significant part of the cost of an art work. To determine the cost of labor, the artist should keep a bound diary -- obtainable in any stationery store -- in which he can record the approximate amount of labor which he has expended on a given project each day that it is under construction. Such a diary can be very useful to curators in later years, for dating an artist's work. But it has a more immediate function for purposes of identifying labor cost elements. If technical or artistic assistants are employed on a project, the cost of their labor should be noted, together with the record of the artist's own labor. Even if labor is volunteered by someone who is anxious to help, the hours donated should be accumulated and evaluated. They should not be passed on to the collector, unintentionally, just because they were contributed to the artist.

Before long, an artist who keeps labor records and studies them occasionally can learn to accurately estimate the approximate number of man hours he needs to produce a work of a given magnitude or to accomplish a given task in preparing such a work. This capability can be very useful in scheduling projects, in budgeting, and in pricing art works. Once all the labor has been accumulated for a particular work, a dollar value should be assigned to the total man hours employed, whether any cash has been paid out for all or part of the labor or not. Failure to evaluate <u>all</u> the labor that has been devoted to creating an art work, because most of this labor was provided by the artist and his friends "without cost," tends to understate the economic value of the work itself. It can lead to improper pricing.

To determine the actual cost of an art work, one must not stop after accumulating the direct cost -- the sum of the value of labor and materials which were employed in making a work. The proceeds of the sale of an art work should also return some appropriate part of the cost of studio rent, utilities, insurance, advertising, business entertainment, etc. These are the "overhead" or operating costs, without which no businessman can operate for long.

Such costs are not easily attributed directly to specific works. Still, an artist who keeps adequate records will discover that he has a certain relatively stable average monthly expense associated with his business operations. This expense can be recovered only through the income produced by the sale of his works. Therefore, in addition to recovering direct costs -- labor and materials -- the artist should identify and recover his indirect -- overhead -- costs.

He may determine these costs for any work by accumulating them and then distributing them appropriately to the individual works which were produced during any given period. For example, if such overhead or operating costs averaged $800 per month over the course of a year, and if the artist expects to sell forty-five or fifty works per year, then he must recover about one-quarter of a month's operating expenses from the sale of each work. In this case, he needs to recover an average of $200 per work to pay for his overhead expenses. In a month where the artist sells fewer works, he will not recover all of his overhead expenses. In a month where he sells more than four works, he should recover more than the cost of such expenses for that month.

Thus, his income can balance out to at least return the artist's costs of doing business through the year. Operating expenses vary from one artist to another, depending on the scope and tempo of each man's activity, but they should always be recovered as a part of the artist's pricing policy.

An alternate method of distributing operating costs functions the same way described above for the distribution of incidental materials costs. If, in the example above, the artist spends an average of forty man-hours making an art work, then he must recover five dollars per man hour to accumulate the necessary $800 from the sale of four works per month. To find his own overhead rate, the artist simply divides the total number of hours devoted to making art during a period into his operating costs for that period.

Several other costs which should be recovered from the sale of an art work remain to be considered. One of these is the cost of the investment which an artist makes in inventory. When an artist works exclusively on commissions and his output is essentially sold before it is finished, he has no significant investment in his works. More often, however, the artist produces a work, holds it in inventory for some time, and subsequently sells it to a dealer or a collector who previously had no

investment in the work. If he gives it to a
dealer on consignment, his investment in the work
continues until a collector is found for it. This
process can require a substantial and continuing
outlay on the part of the artist.

When an investment is made in a savings account,
the depositor can expect to receive interest as well
as federal protection for his funds. If an artist
has invested $500 in creating a work and has held
this work in his inventory for two years, then the
cost of this investment should be considered in his
determination of prices. If, for example, he expects
a modest six percent return on his investment,
then his $500 initial investment should grow in
actual value to $562 over a two year period. This
entire growth in value should be recovered from the
sale of the work. Obviously, the longer a work stays
in inventory the more costly the investment becomes.
We shall return to this question in the discussion of
dealers who work with consigned art works.

A rather ephemeral cost element, but one which should not be overlooked, is the cost of the artist's education. Like any other professional man, an artist must recognize that he has spent a significant portion of his life attaining sufficient technical mastery, insight, and esthetic maturity to produce his works. Renewing these capacities periodically is also a costly feature of the artist's routine development. Such expenditures represent a significant long-term investment, often costing the artist, his family, and society thousands of dollars. Educational costs can best be recovered out of the income which the artist receives from the sale of his work.

Once a work has been produced, unless it was commissioned by a client or otherwise purchased in advance, the artist should anticipate a significant expense associated with locating a collector and selling him the work. Like other costs, the cost of distribution has its own justification and must be recovered from the selling price. Where the artist works on commissions or assignments from collectors, selling costs may be small. Otherwise, showroom space, advertising, and sales effort can be costly.

If the artist -- or his spouse -- functions as his own art dealer, he sometimes fails to recognize that the time spent making contacts, cultivating clients, arranging private sales presentations, exhibiting works, and otherwise engaging in marketing activities embodies a sizeable expenditure. Perhaps, it would be useful if the artist remembers that this same time could be spent creating valuable art works. Marketing work has an identifiable cost, regardless of who does the job.

A gallery operator undertakes to acquire works, hold them in his own inventory, exhibit them, advertise them -- and the artist who produced them -- find clients, encourage the clients to buy, arrange credit, furnish framing and crating, deliver the works to the collectors, to exchange them (in some cases), and perform all the other activities in which an art dealer must engage. When the dealer accomplishes these activities, he is performing a useful service for the artist and for the collector.

In the view of any modern economist, this marketing service adds value to the work. To omit such values from consideration, when the retail price of a work is established, is an unfortunate failure to provide for the recovery of an important part of the total cost of that work. Marketing costs vary, depending on the channel of distribution which is employed, but they should not be ignored.

Finally, the artist must consider the costs of framing, crating, insuring, and delivering the work to the gallery, and to the collector. These costs are generally lumped together as handling charges. They can become quite significant.

In summary, before an artist can recover all of his costs, he must be able to determine what his direct costs for labor and materials were, as well as an appropriate portion of his costs associated with operating his studio. After he has established these costs, he should provide for interest on his investment and for some recovery of the cost of his own education.

He should then determine the cost of selling the work to a collector either directly or through a dealer, and the cost of handling the work as well. Even when all these elements have been included in the price, no profit has been provided for the artist nor has provision been made for the value of the creative image which the work represents. To recover all of the costs mentioned above, for all of the works produced by the artist during the course of a year, is only to break-even during that period. An artist who does not study his costs carefully may not even be breaking-even.

3. Extrinsic Factors - Demand, Supply, Reputation of Artist and Dealer

The most significant considerations, for determining how far _above_ cost a price should be set, are the factors associated with the general interest in, and demand for, an artist's work. Critics and connoisseurs may consider that an art work is moving or otherwise possesses significant esthetic quality. But, unless collectors are _interested_ in acquiring that work, any question of appropriate pricing is simply an academic exercise.

Interest promotes price. Reversing this logic -- a dangerous exercise -- an artist might feel impelled to reduce his prices in order to promote greater interest if there is little demand for his work. But collector interest is probably weak for reasons which have nothing to do with the artist's pricing policy. A badly executed work cannot become more desirable if its price is reduced. More to the point, a properly promoted artist will find that the interest of collectors in his work increases simultaneously with an increase in the prices for his work.

Art dealers generally recognize their obligation to generate demand for the works of the artists which they represent. Accordingly, they should encourage the artist to enter exhibitions and competitions. It is toward this end that they also produce and advertise their own privately sponsored exhibitions of his work. The basic assumption here is that if the work has quality -- as the artist and the dealer suppose it has -- then its systematic exposure to a cultivated public will stimulate demand. This activity serves as a strong support to the artist's pricing structure.

Occasionally, this assumption does not hold. Works are exhibited and may even receive critical acclaim, but they do not always get comparable collector support. This may be due to the dealer's inability to attract the right group of collectors, or it may be due to a certain lassitude in connecting general promotion with more concrete sales activities. On the whole, however, there does seem to be a correlation between the exposure

of works of significant quality and their acceptance
by the collecting public. Exposure stimulates
interest and demand. Demand strengthens prices.

If the interest of collectors is a primary
factor in establishing the price of an art work,
the artist's own reputation may be cited as an
important factor in influencing price because the
growing reputation of the artist usually improves
the demand for his work. Where an artist is
relatively unknown, a dealer might have difficulty
engendering collector interest. Extra effort is
necessary to stimulate adequate demand. On the other
hand, dealers have found that, with an artist of
well-established reputation, one has an easier time
developing interest on the part of collectors even
in a new or unusual image.

The Inelastic Character of Demand for Art

When price increases significantly diminish
the demand for a product or service, economists say
that such a demand is "elastic" with respect to price.

In cases of this kind, the price cannot be
stretched without doing serious damage to the
marketing activity. But, when shifts in price do
not appreciably alter the demand, such a demand
may be considered "inelastic." Characteristically,
the demand for vegetable produce is very elastic.
Each year, as the price of tomatoes rises in the
off-season, housewives tend to buy fewer tomatoes.
As the price drops, they buy more.

But the demand for gasoline has proven
relatively inelastic. Automobile and truck drivers
do not curtail their driving activities significantly
because the price of fuel increases. Also, when
motoring is a bit less expensive, they do not engage
in more driving. While housewives can readily
adjust their interest in salad vegetables to
changing prices, motorists cannot as quickly adjust
their needs for transportation to price fluctuations.

Collectors of art do not tend to buy more works
because prices are down or less frequently when prices

rise. Instead, they often behave like stock

speculators, buying avidly when prices are rising

and losing interest when prices fall or sometimes

even when prices are not advancing steadily. The

artist would do well to think of the price structure

for his works as relatively inelastic in its effect

on demand. Reducing art prices does not improve

demand. Moreover, increasing them, within reasonable

limits, will not necessarily reduce demand.

In fact, as the artist's career matures and

his work gains broader acceptance, his prices should

be expected to increase. In the case of valid work,

this process will continue, hopefully, even after

the artist is no longer living. Certainly not all

artists -- most of whom work in art because they _are_

artists and not primarily because they are seeking

fame or wealth -- can expect to achieve such reknown

that their prices will reach stratospheric proportions.

But every serious artist should recognize that the

increasing price of his own works is, in some sense,

a measure of his continued acceptance by a significant

number of art collectors.

Testing the Market for "le prix juste."

While it is possible to identify and allocate
the costs of producing a work of art with some
precision, the creative talent which lies behind
that work -- determining its esthetic merits --
cannot have a fixed economic value. It is not
possible to determine, with any objectivity,
the ultimate worth of an original and creative
artist's images. Nevertheless, in setting the
price of a work of art, we must try to measure the
relative, if not the objective, dollar value of
the artist's creative effort. One way to do this
involves periodically increasing the prices of his
art works, as collector interest increases --
carefully avoiding drastic or capricious price
increases which might anger or confuse the artist's
following.

An artist should not think of his prices as
fixed, but as based, in good part, on the growing
demand for his works. Some artists and dealers
might hesitate to embark upon a systematic program

of price modification, partly because they fear
that it might result in lost sales and partly
because they find that regular price adjustment
reviews can be bothersome. Nevertheless, if the
artist's work really has significant intrinsic
qualities, and if his clients are increasingly
more attracted to these qualities, then -- as the
artist's reputation and market grows -- his prices
should be periodically increased. Any other course
of action is unfair to the artist and to his dealer.

In the last analysis, it is even harmful to
the interests of his more discerning collectors
who stand to gain as the economic value of their
earlier selections increase -- vindicating their
good judgment and taste. Only when prices are
increased precipitously and without apparent
justification, can this process harm the interests
of the artist, dealer, and collector. As suggested
earlier, the proper starting point for testing the
artist's prices is with his best works. The prices
for these works should be advanced before all others.

Scarcity and Prices

One important ingredient of pricing, which is quite extrinsic to the quality of the work itself, is the relative availability of works by a particular artist or of works from a particular period by that artist. While Rembrandt's works have been widely recognized as masterpieces for many generations, the primary force causing the price of his works to skyrocket in the last few decades has been their increasing scarcity.

Even certain contemporary artists where the output has -- for one reason or another -- generally been low can command a better price for their works than is possible for other artists with a similar interest and demand but a broader supply of works. Thus, the works of Gorky, in short supply for many years, generally fetch a higher price than one might expect to pay for a work of comparable scale and interest by one of his more prolific contemporaries.

So too, the experiences of many artists in the original graphics field indicates that -- all other factors being approximately equal -- an impression from a small edition can command a better price than one from a larger edition. A few short-sighted artists, urged on by avaricious publishers, have recently produced unusually large graphic editions only to find to their dismay that astute collectors question the legitimacy and the technical quality of such works and hesitate to buy them -- even at bargain prices. "Art for the multitude" has been a recurrent slogan for many years, but it is usually associated with low standards of quality and low prices.

In short, scarcity is an important determinant of the price of an artist's work. Artists and their dealers occasionally ignore this relationship and exhibit more works than their own markets can comfortably absorb. For every artist's work there is a balance between supply and demand which is appropriate at a certain point in that artist's career.

A prolific artist might, therefore, be well-advised to hold some of his works off the market until he finds that the demand has become sufficient to justify their release.

Dealers are sometimes alert to such supply-price relationships and intentionally withhold a portion of an artist's oeuvre for sale at a more mature price. The artist seldom shares in this gain, however. As indicated in the section of this text which discusses dealers, there is substantial interest in the development of a marketing system which will permit the artist to participate in the increased prices of his works. Such a system would pay the artist a residual royalty whenever his work is exchanged, just as a performing artist receives a payment when a record, film or tape is sold, broadcast, or reissued.

The Influence of the Artist's Reputation on His Prices

In making selections for their collections, many collectors rely not on their own reaction to the quality of an image, not on their appreciation of the workmanship, nor on their knowledge of the relative merit of different works which are available from different artists. Instead, they depend -- sometimes almost exclusively -- on the reputation of the artist as an index of quality of his work. Such collectors are, of course, courting serious problems. They may not always buy that artist's best works. Nevertheless, reputation is a significant factor in determining prices.

Other collectors, who consider many of the other factors cited here in making their art purchase decisions, are influenced -- even if to a lesser degree -- by the artist's reputation. We seek the approval of others for our decisions in a wide variety of fields. Clearly, an artist whose reputation is vouchsafed by many other collectors and by curators and critics as well must have an image worthy of respect and attention. Given two works of comparable quality, image, and scale, the collector will generally pay more for the work created by the better-known artist.

So too, we are influenced by the reputations of certain dealers who are well known for their leadership in various schools of art. The fact that an artist's work is carried by such a dealer may enhance the collector's willingness to buy and strengthen the price he is willing to pay.

Price Ranges for Groups of Collectors

Works by artists of a given reputation, medium, and level of interest are often lumped together mentally by certain collectors who regularly buy in a narrow price range. A collector may be accustomed to paying from $500 to $750 for an oil of a particular size by a contemporary artist who has a certain modest reputation in the art world.

If this collector is shown an interesting work by such an artist at a price well below this range, he may hesitate to buy. Perhaps he will suspect that his own judgment regarding the work is defective -- that "something must be wrong." Or he may simply be unable to focus on a work which is "below" his level of interest.

If, on the other hand, the same collector is shown such a work, and the price quoted is considerably above his expectations, he may decide to buy another work which is more in keeping with his own buying habits and which he finds just as attractive as the first work. Or he may put off a buying decision entirely. He is using his narrow price range as a gauge within which to make his purchase decisions.

Thus, the collector can impose a certain amount of price restraint upon himself through exercising his notion of a range within which prices are appropriate for certain classes of work by certain groups of artists. This restraint works two ways.

He tends to reject works which he feels are priced "too low," as well as those which he finds priced "too high." Years later, he may sigh over some important but lost purchase opportunity. But the habit of buying within the narrow price range persists.

I once met a very wealthy, otherwise astute collector who confided that it was his policy to never pay more than $1,000 for an art work -- no matter whose. While he had a good collection -- because his tastes were sound -- he had lost the chance to buy many great works, including some which he sorely regretted passing up. I understand that James Johnson Sweeney once advised an inter-mediate collector to always try to buy works which are a little more expensive than he could afford. This wise dictum stretches the collector's aspirations as well as his purse.

"Competitive" Prices

In setting their prices, some artists rely rather heavily on the guidance offered by prevailing prices asked for the works of other artists. As indicated above, there is a certain degree of logic to this. Collectors within a community may have accustomed themselves to certain price-range limitations regarding works of a particular character. However, artists and their works are seldom in direct competition with each other. If the works are truly the expressions of individuals, then they are not strictly comparable.

Occasionally, artists will indeed compete for a commission, but seldom is one artist granted a commission over another because his price was lower.* On the other hand, art collectors seldom think of their avocation as an inexpensive or money-

---

*However, the artist who enters a bid for a commission in competition with other artists would be well advised to try to base his price, at least in part, on what he thinks the other artists will ask. If not, he might find his price far beyond the jury's budget or far too modest.

saving activity. I can think of no cases where collectors have ever described themselves as "price comparison" art buyers.

The importance of "meeting" competition in establishing the price of an art work is probably overstated. Collectors do not buy works simply because they are available at competitive prices. Prices asked by other artists are useful then primarily as a possible starting point for establishing a price structure for an artist's own works. They may also serve as limits on a dealer whose clients have adjusted themselves to a preconceived notion of that dealer's prices. But the prices for the works of two artists are seldom really competitive.

Clearance Sales and Discounting Practices

From time to time, artists and dealers have raised the question of the propriety of such well-known merchandising activities as clearance sales,

price cutting, and discounting in the field of
art. I can think of no case where a clearance
sale serves to enhance the long term interests
of an artist. Certainly, a dealer who performs
a valuable marketing function for an artist is
entitled to receive a wholesale trade discount
from the artist or from another dealer. These
are established discounts, below the retail price.
From this discount, the purchasing dealer must
recoup his own costs and support his own establishment.

But the policy some artists and dealers follow,
of giving discounts to friends, collectors, and
institutions is harmful to the interests of the
artist, since it undermines his price structure.
It sets up two categories of customers: insiders,
who can buy at "wholesale" rates, and outsiders,
who must pay full price. Later on, the outsider
may become justifiably angry when he discovers that
his friends have received preferential price treatment. Wholesale rates should be reserved for
wholesale transactions. Why an institution should

expect preferential treatment is beyond me --

considering that the cost of making such a sale

is generally greater than the cost of a sale to

an ordinary collector.

There is one condition where a special

pricing policy is indeed justified by the nature

of the transaction. The merits of special pricing

treatment in this case are recognized in the

Robinson-Patman Act, the federal legislation which

is designed to prevent unfair price discrimination.

A collector who buys many works at a time may be

entitled to a better price per work than a collector

who buys only a single work at a time. This is fair

because serving the client who buys in large volume

generally requires a lower cost of sales per work

than serving a man who buys only one or two works

at a time. Some artists reduce their prices by as much

as ten percent when the total value of a single

transaction exceeds five thousand dollars. For

the same reason, original graphics artists often

set the price of their suites ten percent below

their prices for individual impressions of comparable quality.

But all other discounting practices which seek to give special consideration to certain classes of customers -- without regard to relative selling costs -- are probably illegal. They are certainly unwise because they materially reduce the possibility that the artist can support himself with the sale of his work. They are a form of subsidy to favored collectors.

Pricing the Artist's Services

Artists are occasionally employed or commissioned by a client to create a work of art or to design and supervise the creation of a work where the client expects to pay all material and incidental costs as they are incurred. The artist's relationship to the client, from the point of view of pricing, is in this case radically different from his role as an artist who produces his works for subsequent display and sale. Where he has only his own labor

and his own creative talent to sell, while all
expenses are to be paid by the client, the
artist's profit opportunity may be considerably
reduced -- just as his investment and risk has
been reduced.

Often such arrangements are negotiated on
a fixed-price basis. Occasionally, they may also
be made on some sort of time-oriented or percentage-
of-costs basis. If the artist accepts a fixed-price
commission, he should be sure that he has carefully
estimated all the time required to do the work and
has properly established the intrinsic value of
the creative activity which will be needed. Comparing
his price to the fee he might earn during this
period as a teacher is improper and irrelevant.

One way to determine an appropriate price for
the artist's services is to develop a price which
would be appropriate if such a work were being sold
to a collector after its completion. From this
amount, the artist can subtract the estimated cost

of materials, assistance labor, overhead, and other
elements which are to be furnished by the client.
The remainder might be an appropriate price for the
artist's services.

When the artist is paid by the hour, week or
month, he should remember that during this time,
he is performing a creative function as well as a
supervisory and labor function. Since he is not
simply a mechanic, following a blueprint which has
been prepared by someone else, he must take into
account the higher value of his own creative activities.
Again, in order to test the validity of his pricing
policy, he should compare his anticipated price with
the net income after all expenses are recovered
which he would generate if he were selling finished
works produced during this same time period.

Pricing Under the French Point System

Many European art dealers, and a few in the
United States, price the works of their artists on
the basis of the French Point System. Each work

is assigned a certain number of points, based on its scale. For each artist represented by a gallery, a dollar or franc value is assigned to one point. The price of an individual work is then a matter of simple arithmetic.

This system has the virtue of being internally consistent. Any clerk can determine the correct number of points for a given work and can then calculate the price. But, it does not give recognition to the vast differences in quality which occur, not uncommonly, within an artist's oeuvre -- even within a period. Since these differences are not considered, the system can produce prices which are not true reflections of intrinsic merit.

However, even if this problem were resolved, we could still not avoid a number of significant difficulties. Not the least of these is the task of determining the value of the point. For this we must fall back upon the considerations discussed earlier. If we omit consideration of intrinsic merit, cost recovery and such extrinsic factors as reputation

and demand, how are we to establish the value of
a point for a particular artist? But, when we
have considered these issues carefully, what added
purpose does the point system serve?

The Effect of Credit on Pricing

In the modern credit economy which has
developed in this culture over the past five decades,
it is curious that the artist and the art dealer
have no clear cut credit practices. Art works are
often too expensive for even fairly affluent
collectors, if they are asked to pay cash for them.

A fairly large number of art dealers proudly
offer credit terms to their collectors at no cost,
neglecting to note that the works so distributed
are not their own property -- but are consigned to
them by their artists. I feel that offering "free"
credit is always a dubious practice. Offering works
which are not the dealer's own property to collectors --
without adequate recompense to the artist -- is an
outrageous assault on modern business methods.

Every consumer understands that credit is
an expensive privelege -- not easily obtained
and _never_ rendered without cost. If a collector
is not required to pay appropriate interest
charges for the credit rendered to him by a dealer,
he has little reason to believe that the price of
the art work does not already include a certain
charge for credit. The major merchandising firms
have found that the addition of clearly stated
credit charges does not diminish their business --
as some had thought it might. It works the other
way around, encouraging many consumers to buy
merchandise they could otherwise not afford.

Where a merchant is too small to develop and
install his own credit system, he may easily affiliate
with any of a number of widely-held credit card
systems such as Master-Charge, Carte Blanche, and
Bankamericard. In these cases, the larger agency
pays the merchant (often at a discounted rate) and
then collects directly from the client -- charging
no interest for prompt payment.

I find that those art dealers who offer such
credit facilities to their collectors meet no
appreciable resistance when they withdraw their
earlier "free credit" terms. I see no reason
why an individual artist cannot offer a similar
opportunity to his clients.

A CHECKLIST OF FACTORS RELATED TO
THE ARTIST'S PRICING POLICIES

The problem of pricing is one of recognizing values under rather subjective circumstances. This too is an art which must be cultivated before it can be practiced successfully. Prices for art work should <u>recover costs, measure intrinsic merit</u>, and <u>test the demand</u> for the artist's image and reputation as well as the <u>available supply</u> of his work. Since these are dynamic forces, the prices to which they give rise must be reviewed and modified frequently.

The appended checklist is not inclusive of every pricing problem nor is it a "formula" for establishing prices. But it can act as a series of unweighted reminders which the artist and his dealer should discuss and consider regularly when they establish and review prices for art works. At various times and circumstances, different elements of this checklist will become relatively more or less significant in determining the appropriate price of a particular work or the range of prices of works within a collection.

I. INTRINSIC QUALITIES

A. Esthetic Factors   Check One

    (1) Collectors with a particular esthetic
        interest or bias will appreciate
        these works.   ( )

    (2) These works are examples of an art
        movement or school which has attracted
        the interest of a significant number
        of collectors.   ( )

    (3) These works are representative of the
        oeuvre of a well-known artist.   ( )

    (4) These works are the best examples
        available by a moderately well-established
        artist.   ( )

    (5) These are among the best available works
        by a very well-known artist.   ( )

B. Technological Factors

    (1) The technical quality of these works is
        sound. Materials employed are standard
        or better and methods used are acceptable.   ( )

    (2) These works are well-constructed and
        properly mounted or framed. Materials
        are of high quality.   ( )

    (3) These works have been attractively
        mounted or framed and are composed of
        very high quality materials. The artist
        employed unusually fine, painstaking
        techniques in executing his concept.   ( )

II. COST RECOVERY

		Yes	No
		(X)	
(1)	The cost of all the <u>materials</u> directly employed in making these works has been carefully calculated.	( )	( )
(2)	The artist's <u>labor</u> and any labor furnished by assistants or volunteers has been evaluated at established rates.	( )	( )
(3)	An allowance has been made to recover an appropriate share of the artist's studio rent, utilities, insurance, and similar <u>overhead</u> costs.	( )	( )
(4)	The cost of carrying the works in <u>inventory</u> have been calculated.	( )	( )
(5)	The cost of the artist's <u>education</u> have been considered.	( )	( )
(6)	The anticipated cost of <u>promoting</u> and <u>selling</u> these works has been distributed equitably to the estimated total cost of each work. This includes provision for the salesman's commission (if any) and for a share of the gallery's operating expenses.	( )	( )
(7)	The cost of <u>handling</u> these works, including crating, framing, and shipping (in and out) has been identified and included.	( )	( )

III. EXTRINSIC FACTORS

A. Demand: Collector Interest

Check One

(1) These works were not created by a well-established artist. They currently generate sporadic collector interest. ( )

(2) These works are not by a well-established artist. They currently arouse modest, but fairly consistent collector interest. ( )

(3) These works are by a fairly well-established artist. Nevertheless, collector interest in them has been rather modest. ( )

(4) These works are by a well-established artist. Collector interest is fairly strong. ( )

(5) These works are by a well-established artist. Collector demand often exceeds the available supply of this artist's works. ( )

B. Artist's Reputation

(1) The artist has no significant following of collectors. ( )

(2) The artist has a small but loyal following of collectors, each of whom owns two or more of his works. ( )

(3) The artist is rapidly increasing his reputation through awards, acceptance in juried shows, critical reviews of one-man shows, and sales to collectors. ( )

(4) The artist's reputation has been well-established for some time among a significant number of collectors and critics. ( )

(5) The artist is a leading force in contemporary art. ( )

EXTRINSIC FACTORS, cont'd.

C. <u>Scarcity</u>   <u>Check One</u>

    (1) The artist's works are available in
        a quantity which exceeds the actual
        demand by collectors.   ( )

    (2) The artist's works are readily available
        in a variety of images and moods, but
        demand can be expected to closely approach
        supply over the next few years.   ( )

    (3) Demand for the artist's works are growing
        much faster than the supply of new and
        pre-existing works.   ( )

    (4) The artist's works have historically been
        in short supply. Collector demand is great. ( )

    (5) The artist's works, while very attractive
        to collectors, will always be in short
        supply for technical reasons or because
        the artist's output is low.   ( )

D. <u>Dealer's Reputation</u>

    (1) The dealer is not well enough established
        to significantly stimulate interest in
        the artist's works.   ( )

    (2) The dealer is fairly well-respected as a
        source for works of considerable esthetic
        interest.   ( )

    (3) The dealer is able to add significantly
        to collector interest in the artist's
        works because of his broad reputation
        and good contacts.   ( )

    (4) The dealer can place the artist's works
        in important collections without too
        much trouble.   ( )

    (5) The dealer's reputation and affiliations are
        such that he can sell all the valid works
        the artist can deliver.   ( )

EXTRINSIC FACTORS, cont'd.

E. Competitive Prices   <u>Check One</u>

    (1) The works are comparable in scale and
        quality to those of certain artists
        in a particular gallery.   ( )

    (2) The works are comparable in scale and
        quality to those of certain artists
        in a particular community or trend in art. ( )

    (3) The works are not really comparable for
        pricing purposes with other art works
        available in this area, except perhaps
        in terms of the reputation of the artist.   ( )

F. Discount and Credit Policy

    (1) A wholesale discount policy has been
        established.   ( )

    (2) A volume discount policy has been
        established.   ( )

    (3) Special interest discounts are
        prohibited.   ( )

    (4) A credit policy has been established.   ( )

IV. PERIODIC REVIEW AND REVISION

		Yes (X)	No
(1)	Prices have been systematically adjusted to reflect shifts in the value of money and changes in the cost of living.	( )	( )
(2)	Prices currently asked for the artist's works have recently been compared with and adjusted to prices for the works of other artists whose works provoke comparable interest and demand.	( )	( )
(3)	Prices currently asked for the artist's works have recently been adjusted to reflect a measurable increase in demand for the artist's work.	( )	( )
(4)	Prices for certain particularly interesting or important works have been adjusted upward to "test the market," by determining whether collector resistance will be met at the newly selected price level.	( )	( )
(5)	Prices have been increased to reflect a shift in the balance between growing demand and diminishing supply.	( )	( )

DEALERS

Selecting a Dealer

As suggested earlier, a curious and unfortunate disproportion exists in the United States today between the rather small number of art dealers capable of representing contemporary artists and the comparatively large number of good artists who are seeking such representation. Further, the number of potential collectors in the United States today far exceeds the capabilities of existing art dealers as well.

Not every business which calls itself an art gallery is able or willing to represent the contemporary artist. Many of these firms might be more properly described as "picture stores," specializing in the sale of low cost, decorative pictures and frames. Another large group of galleries is not primarily directed at representing relatively new contemporary U.S. artists but has concentrated instead on trading the works of very

well-established artists of this and earlier eras.
Neither of these groups is willing to invest a
great deal of effort or money in developing the
careers of contemporary artists.

In the New York area, more than 800 businesses
describe themselves as art galleries. Fewer than
400 of these actually represent any significant
number of contemporary U.S. artists. Since a gallery
usually handles only ten to twenty artists at any
time, it may be seen that fewer than 6,000 living
American artists are represented by the entire New York
art dealing community. Some of these institutions are
"vanity" galleries which do very little selling but
offer exhibition space to artists for a fee.

The situation is even more difficult in other
markets. Los Angeles and Chicago are among the largest
art markets outside of the New York area. In each
of these communities, fewer than 100 dealers actively
represent contemporary artists. In communities such
as Detroit, Dallas, Cleveland and San Francisco,

the number of galleries devoting their attention
to contemporary art is even smaller. As a rough
approximation, it seems reasonable to conclude
that not more than 12,000 artists are currently
represented by art dealers and many are poorly
represented at that.

On the other hand, by any measure, there are
tens of thousands of artists who, for one reason
or another, have no gallery representation. Some
of these are represented by the "picture stores,"
by cooperative artists' associations, and by other
relatively less effective marketing institutions.

One surprisingly effective method of representation for contemporary artists is through the private
art dealer. These enterprising businessmen generally
sell works from a small office or in their own homes.
They emphasize private sales presentations and avoid
public exhibitions. I have no statistics on the
number of such specialists, but the group appears
to be growing in many communities and prospering,
as well.

Still, most artists simply have no sales representation at all, regardless of the quality of their image or the potential demand for their work. The opportunity for new galleries is great if their founders can find a way to cultivate and satisfy and potential demands of collectors through a combination of good taste, hard work, and adequate working capital. The greatest opportunity is of course to be found outside of the major metropolitan areas in high income communities of moderate size.

For the present, however, the artist must realize that he is looking for representation in a market where good dealers are at a premium. If the artist's image is new, exciting, arresting, it may be possible for him to find representation in a gallery which devotes itself to promoting avant-garde images. If the artist's image is interesting but somewhat more conventional, he must compete with many other artists who are creating good but relatively familiar images.

Earlier in this text, it was proposed that
one very reasonable way of overcoming the competitive
disadvantages which a new artist faces in seeking
representation involves building a reputation and
a clientele _outside_ of the galleries. These
factors can provide a good foundation for subsequently finding a reliable dealer. Thus, if a
dealer is shown works and slides by an artist whose
work shows competence and interest, he may or may
not be moved to accept that artist for representation
by his gallery, depending on his needs and his
available capital. If, in addition, he finds that
the artist has already successfully entered important
competitions, exhibited in significant juried shows,
and has established a clientele in the dealer's own
marketing area, that dealer's interest in representing
such an artist should be increased significantly.

To find a dealer within any particular art market,
the artist should engage in a little market research.
First, he should prepare a list of those dealers who
presently represent artists with images and reputations

which are generally compatible to his own. Clearly,
an artist whose work involves optical effects or
surrealistic symbols will be wasting his own time
and that of the dealer if he contacts a gallery
owner whose main interest is in more conventional
images.

To develop this list, he might review the listing in
his local Yellow Pages directory or he might consult
the local art calendar, if one is published. He should
cull this preliminary listing by visiting the galleries
to examine the works which they show. There is not
much sense in making a presentation to a gallery which
emphasizes famous artists unless the artist seeking
placement has a comparable claim. So. too, he should
evaluate the other artists represented by the gallery.
Their images should be at least generally compatible
with his.

Once an artist has compiled and edited a list
of potential dealers, he should send each gallery
a letter requesting an interview and enclosing a
one or two page resume. This resume should contain

the artist's name, age, address, telephone, and media. It should also contain a summary of his art education, showing schools attended and the years in which he was at these schools, together with the names of any significant artists with whom he has studied. A separate section should list exhibitions and competitions with which he has been successfully involved, together with dates and prizes. Another section should list the names of significant public and private collections in which the artist's work may be found.

The letter and resume should be followed by a telephone call to set up an appointment. As in the case of selling the artist's work, this call has the purpose of "qualifying" the prospect -- in this case the art dealer. Some dealers are very courteous and may be willing to see the artist, even though they cannot possibly undertake to represent any new artists for the next few years. The artist should determine the capability of the dealer for handling promising new artists before he finalizes the appointment. This can save him a good deal of wasted time.

At the appointment, the artist should show his
work as he would to a collector, remembering, however,
that the dealer may know a good deal more about art
than many collectors. If the dealer is interested
in the work, the artist should discuss sales
representation first and exhibition second. He may
tell the dealer about the number of collectors who
already own more than one of his works in the dealer's
marketing area. He should also show him any significant
critical notices which his work has received.

He should ask the dealer how he works with his
other artists and whether he is prepared to make an
investment of time and money in the artist's work.
If the dealer decides that he is not interested in
handling the work at this time, the artist might ask
him for suggestions regarding other dealers who might
react differently. If the dealer is interested in
handling the work, the artist should offer to help him
to contact collectors of his own who might be
interested in examining recent works in private sales
presentations at the gallery.

The relationship between artist and dealer should be formalized and reduced to writing at this point -- even if it is a trial agreement. As indicated later on in this section of the text, even the content of a casual consignment agreement covering only a few works deserves to be reduced to writing.

The Dealer's Investment

Any dealer who undertakes to sell an artist's works must plan to make a certain investment in introducing the artist to his clientele. The minimum level at which a gallery can invest in an artist's work includes participation in the cost of an exhibition and a certain amount of direct mail and other advertising to encourage attendance at that exhibition. Some dealers ask their artists to share in these costs, usually out of the first proceeds of sales arising from the exhibition.

Dealers in our principal art markets find that it costs them from $300 to $750 for relatively modest publicity on an exhibition held in their gallery. To this must be added the cost of properly hanging the exhibition and of operating the gallery, in terms of rent, utilities, insurance and manpower. Even a simple three week exhibition in a dealer's gallery has an effective cost of $500 to $1,500. To undertake this investment, the dealer should have some expectation of either immediate or early future sales.

An intelligent dealer will not undertake the representation of an artist unless he can afford to invest considerably more than the cost of an exhibition, which is, after all, a relatively short-term investment, if it generates sufficient volume to cover its cost. Such dealers may wish to purchase certain works outright from the artist, or they may advance funds against anticipated earnings from the sale of the artist's work. A dealer may go even further, placing his artists under some form of contract with guaranteed monthly payments or guaranteed annual sales. In each of these cases, since the investment level differs, the proportion of the sales dollar retained by the gallery may be increased.

Where the dealer makes a very small investment, taking works only on consignment, his share in the proceeds of sales have historically amounted to one-third. But, a study of the financial records of a number of different art dealers shows that such an arrangement is seldom profitable for the dealer. The cost of operating a small or medium-sized gallery generally runs between thirty percent and thirty-five percent of sales income, without providing any return on investment to the dealer or even any compensation for his time.

Accordingly, a number of dealers have recently decided that they should retain forty percent of the income from the sale of consigned art works. A few dealers even demand fifty percent discounts on consigned works, but this seems a wholly unwarranted

proportion, considering their lack of investment.
Where the dealer has actually made a substantial
investment, either through his outright purchase
of works or through advances or fixed payments
(stipends) to the artist, the dealer generally
retains fifty percent of the selling price -- a
portion to which he is usually entitled by virtue
of his effort and risk.

Of course, there is a stronger incentive to sell
the work of an artist when the dealer has a
significant investment in it. The artist should bear
this in mind if he is negotiating with a dealer who
handles some works which he owns and others which he
holds on consignment. It is very difficult for a
dealer to be unbiased about works which he already
owns and which will pay him a better rate of profit.
One solution which a number of well-known artists
have found to the problem is to insist that the
dealer must maintain a certain minimum investment
level in their works. This practice is very common

in other kinds of marketing, where a merchant
is required to maintain a minimum investment in
the merchandise of his supplier in order to
qualify for the status of "dealer."

Where the artist's negotiating position is
strong because of his well-established reputation
and existing clientele, he would be wise to insist
upon a relatively substantial level of investment
as the basis of a dealer representation agreement.
Some artists tend to concentrate their attention on
their desire for gallery exhibitions every year or
every two years. While such gallery exhibitions
can be helpful to the artist's career, they are not
substitutes for the prestige associated with the
artist's participation in important museum shows or
national and regional competitions.

Gallery exhibitions are seldom as useful in developing
an artist's career. One-man museum shows are, of course,
relatively very prestigious. A dealer can occasionally
stimulate such exhibitions. But the dealer's most
important function is to sell -- not to show. The

main emphasis of his efforts should focus on this
issue.

The Artist's Residual Rights

The artist may retain certain rights often
associated with the sale of his works. In some
states, he automatically retains the right to
control the reproduction of his images by others,
even after he has sold the original. Even where
the law does not provide this protection, he may
obtain it simply by registering a copyright claim
with the Department of Copyrights at the Library
of Congress in Washington -- an inexpensive procedure --
and then by specifically excluding the transfer of his
properly advertised copyright from the sale of the work.

The artist may also attempt to retain certain
property rights regarding subsequent transfers of
title of his works. Ed Keinholz has done this in
recent years. So too, Seth Siegelaub has recently
been urging artists to consider asking their collectors

to sign an Agreement for Transfer of Work of Art
(copies obtainable by writing to P.O. Box 350,
New York 10013). This agreement is examined in
detail in the April, 1971 issue of Art News. It
provides for payment of a portion of the
appreciated value of an art work to the artist
whenever a transfer of title is made.

It is my own opinion that such agreements are
reasonable and fair, but that they will work best
when someone establishes a central title registry
to monitor title changes the way motor vehicle and
real property title changes are monitored. I believe
that this could be done on a voluntary, non-government
basis by a non-profit agency like Artist's Equity.

Other Markets - Other Galleries

Once an artist has become fairly well-established
in one market area, he should consider expanding into
others. Again, the competition for representation
in the better galleries is keen. But the fact that

an artist is doing well in Chicago should be meaningful to a dealer in Cleveland or Baltimore.

One sure way to find acceptance involves building up a clientele and a reputation in the new city. If the artist enters local competitions, meets collectors and curators and generally builds a reputation and a following in that community, he will, once again, find dealer acceptance is more readily available. This generally means that the artist must travel to the city in question, perhaps in conjunction with exhibitions or museum shows. He might also visit the city as an invited artist-in-residence at a local art college. On these occasions, he should send advance letters to local collectors announcing his visit and he should seek local publicity regarding his arrival. After establishing his esthetic and marketing credentials in a community, the artist may seek gallery representation with greater assurance of success.

Care should be exercised to avoid conflicting market territories. Thus, if a New York dealer is representing an artist, he may or may not cover that artist's clients in northern New Jersey or Philadelphia. The limits of a dealer's selling territory should be defined at the outset in the dealer's agreement.

A market has developed for some U.S. artists in Europe, Asia, and Latin America. Occasionally, the artist's most important U.S. dealer can help to establish representation in foreign galleries. More often, however, the artist must make his own contacts, first by mail and later in person. In a few instances, foreign dealers travel to the United States to select new artists. As important as it is in this country, it is even more important to keep agreements with foreign dealers in writing. To avoid misunderstandings and losses, the artist should do business only with well-established business institutions.

Dealing with Dealers

Most artists in the United States maintain rather
informal business relationships with their dealers.
Few ever bother committing to writing the agreements
under which they distribute their works. They seem
to be unaware of the many different kinds of
arrangements which are available, much less the
underlying reasons for each of these approaches.

Lacking any other frame of reference for their
dealings, artists often accept the first business
proposal made to them by a dealer, disregarding its
subtler or even its onerous implications. As the
artist's career develops, he may find his relationship
with his dealer has become inappropriate or self-
defeating because it was not well thought out in
the first place. At this late stage, he has the
choice of trying to negotiate better terms or of
starting out all over again to find a new dealer.
But disengagement from the old dealer can be a
mutually damaging process. Collectors are not readily
transferred from one dealer to another and few artists
acquire new collectors without considerable effort.

The artist needs a dealer only in terms of specific functions which he can perform. And the dealer needs the artist for the works which he can create and for the business which his works can generate. Thus, there can be a fruitful and symbiotic business association between the artist and the dealer at many levels. But failure to set down the terms of the relationship clearly and fully -- so that misunderstandings are minimized -- often results in bruised feelings, anger, and lost opportunities. Many otherwise valid dealer-artist arrangements have foundered because they were not worked out carefully in advance and in writing.

The Dealer's Functions

The first question to be answered is: <u>Which functions will the dealer perform?</u> A dealer may perform many different tasks depending upon his own abilities and interests, the qualities of his artists' work, the level of development of his clientele, and his own financial condition.

Fundamentally, he will be performing a sales function --
that is, he will be offering the artist's works for
sale to private collectors and to institutions in a
given market area.

To be sure, there are a few exceptions where the
dealer's function is <u>not</u> primarily one of selling works,
but of supervising "happenings" or helping to create
"environments." In this sense, however, the dealer
is more a producer of entertainment of one kind or
another -- as the artist shifts from the graphic arts
to the performing arts. But the graphic or plastic
artist is primarily a creator of substantive works
which may be viewed, appreciated, and, of course,
<u>purchased</u>.

In addition to the dealer's task of finding and
cultivating collectors for the artist's existing work,
the dealer may or may not also:

(1) <u>Arrange and negotiate commission
agreements with architects and others</u> leading to the
subsequent preparation of works specifically designed
to fill a client's need. When he does so, he often

receives a relatively small percentage of the
artist's fee for his efforts. Two commonly
encountered rates for this service are ten percent
of the selling price or twenty percent of the
artist's net fee -- the sum which is left after
deducting the total cost of producing the work
from the selling price. Percentages, here and
elsewhere, can be deceiving. A larger percentage
may yield less after deductions than a smaller
percentage without deductions.

(2) <u>Coordinate the financing of an art
commission by others</u>, such as the commissioning
agent or some third party. This function may be
a regular part of the dealer's work as a commission
agent or it may be needed only in special cases.

(3) <u>Arrange, install and publicize gallery
exhibitions</u> of the artist's work, in group and in
one-man shows. For many dealers, this is the most
time-consuming and expensive activity involved in
operating a gallery. Artists and their dealers often

overexpend their resources seeking public exposure in the gallery, leaving little time or money for other equally important functions, such as cultivating potential clients intensively.

(4) <u>Arrange and publicize museum and travelling exhibitions</u> where the artist's work is featured or where it is an integral component of a larger show.

(5) <u>Promote the artist's reputation, his views, and his works</u> through advertising campaigns and through publicity programs. Carefully developed promotional campaigns are often the key to the success of a contemporary artist.

(6) <u>Produce brochures, art books, films</u> and other publications regarding the artist's work. Such activities can be partially self-supporting and they can significantly enhance the career of an artist, making his image widely available to many who might otherwise have relatively little contact with it. While this activity does not always directly stimulate the sale of art works, it tends to increase their salability because it makes the artist's image better known.

(7) <u>Submit the artist's work</u> to juried shows and competitions. This function may be overlooked by the more complacent dealer who is not always too alert to opportunities for expanding his artist's area of public contact. But it is important to the development of the career of a relatively unknown artist.

(8) <u>Arrange for the rental of the artist's works</u> for long or short terms. This activity is of particular significance for major works. Some institutions prefer a lease financing agreement to an outright purchase becuase they can treat their lease payments as business expenses while purchases must be capitalized and this requires slower depreciation treatment.

(9) <u>Arrange and finance collateral services</u>, such as crating, framing, delivery, insurance, and shipping, for the artist's work. The appropriate approach to such services might be discussed with the artist but the costs should be passed on to the customer.

(10) <u>Extend credit</u> to qualified collectors of the artist's works. As indicated elsewhere, the cost of this service and the risks should not be absorbed by the artist but rather passed on to the client.

(11) <u>Purchase specific works</u> from the artist from time to time at an established discount rate. In the case of an artist whose work is increasing in value, an astute dealer can earn substantial profits for himself by buying works and holding certain of them until their value has increased. A few dealers have begun to share some of this appreciation with their artists.

(12) <u>Issue periodic cash advances</u> to the artist against his future earnings or against an annual guaranteed income level. This function requires good capital resources and a great measure of self-confidence from the dealer, but it is a very desirable condition for the artist and might justify payment of a higher commission rate to the dealer.

Some Problems of Consigning Art Works

All of these activities, with the exception of
the first two, involve the dealer in certain
financial commitments. They also presume skill,
experience, and the proper utilization of time
and contacts by the dealer. Generally, the first
ten of these functions are less costly than the
last two. These require regular cash outlays to
the artist or outright purchases of the artist's
works. Since there are few framers, job printers,
insurance companies, or shipping firms willing to
speculate regarding when or whether they are to be
paid for their services, the first ten functions
are generally conducted on a cash basis or on a
short-term credit arrangement.

To help resolve their operating cash problems,
many dealers insist on accepting works from artists
only, or primarily, on consignment. This policy
usually includes a reduced sales commission to the
dealer. But it creates conditions which the artist
often finds self-defeating. When the dealer insists

on a consignment of the artist's works, he is
impairing the ability of both artist and dealer
to function properly.

The consigning artist is, in effect, financing
his dealer's inventory. Such practices are seldom
found in other merchandising fields, today. Thus,
diamond merchants, jewelers, and antique dealers
do not ask their suppliers to underwrite their
inventories, although such firms are undoubtedly
more capable of performing this function than most
contemporary artists.

Dealers tend to favor works which they own over
consigned works, for reasons of their own economic
interest. When a dealer sells a work he owns, he
is liquidating his own investment and earning a
good profit. When he sells the artist's work, he
is obtaining a smaller profit and liquidating the
artist's investment.

Also, the artist's control over his works is
weak when they are being held on consignment.
Insurance coverage is harder to arrange. He may
find himself unpaid for works that were actually

sold months earlier. In the event of the dealer's

death or bankruptcy, his ownership of the works

may be contested by the dealer's heirs or creditors.

At its best, it is doubtful whether the

difference in trade discount rates allowed for

purchased works as compared to consigned works is

sufficient compensation for the artist's investment

in the dealer. This usually amounts to between ten

and thirteen percent. If a consigned work is held

by a dealer for two years before it is sold, and,

if the artist then receives sixty percent of the

selling price -- compared to a fifty percent discount

which the same artist might have allowed on a cash

sale -- we have a situation where the dealer is

paying the artist less than five percent per year

for the use of the artist's money.

A savings institution pays its clients more.

A department store typically gets eighteen percent

per year when it gives credit. But when an artist

consigns a work with a selling price of $1,000 to a

dealer, he may receive $600 when it is sold instead

of $500 which he would have allowed in an outright sale. Thus, he has effectively "charged" the dealer $100 for the use of his inventory. Over a two year period, this averages to $50 per year. If the dealer borrowed $500 from a bank to buy the work and paid current bank rates, his costs -- compounded -- would be higher.

These calculations do not even consider the possibility that the work may not be sold at all, in which case the artist's investment would be tied up indefinitely. Consignment selling is not, in the last analysis, a fruitful or mutually beneficial arrangement. It is neither wise nor productive for a little-known artist, and it is quite unwarranted for an established artist, whose works sell consistently.

Nevertheless -- where an artist is new to a gallery -- the dealer may wish to engage himself minimally with a few selected works to see whether he can sell them. As his experience and clientele grows, he may want to shift to a different kind of relationship -- one in which he has the benefit of a

much broader inventory of works in exchange for a
fixed monthly payment.

This payment may be simply an advance against
the artist's future earnings, or more desirably,
it may be some form of guaranteed income. In
either case, the payment should not provide for
transfer of any ownership until a specific work
has been sold. The dealer is acting as a "sales
agent" for the artist. Ownership actually transfers
directly from the artist to the collector. If he
has provided an annual guarantee, the dealer may wish
to reserve the right to apply his unearned advances,
if any, against his own subsequent purchase of
specific works annually or semi-annually when accounts
are reconciled.

But most of the works which come into the
dealer's care are not actually his own. Whether
the dealer has made cash payments or guarantees to
the artist or not, clarifying ownership of the works
submitted to his care is a critical issue. In the
absence of contrary agreements and properly executed

and recorded legal notices, the dealer's creditors and heirs may assume that any works which he exhibits and offers for sale are his property. The burden is on the artist to prove otherwise.

Again, although the dealer does not own most of the works in his care, he should be responsible for the insurance of these works against fire or theft. While it is theoretically possible for the artist to carry a "floater" to protect his works, such insurance is seldom practical or economical.

Finally, the artist needs a clear statement regarding the issuance of credit to collectors and regarding the basis of settlement between the artist and the dealer. The dealer who holds the artist's work on consignment usually has many unsettled business obligations toward that artist.

Why Write Up The Artist/Dealer Agreement?

The artist who does not have a written agreement with his dealer, may, nevertheless, have entered into a legally binding contract without realizing it. The courts have generally held that whenever two parties engage in transactions where one or both are accomplishing certain specific, previously agreed upon tasks or services, and where a consideration is involved, a contract exists, objectively, until it is mutually revoked. The basic elements of a contract, <u>viz</u>: an offer by one party to perform certain functions, an acceptance of that offer, by another party, and a price or some other form of payment to bind the deal, need not be reduced to writing to constitute a valid contract.

Some artists have also -- without realizing it -- become business partners of gallery operators in "joint ventures." Again, a written partnership agreement is not a legal necessity -- but it is certainly more useful than a series of verbal under-standings which more often than not lead to serious misunderstandings.

Failure to consider fully and explicitly the terms of an agreement can lead to confusion, disagreement, and litigation. The artist who fails to insist upon a written agreement is simply increasing his chances for trouble as a businessman. He would be well-advised to seek the help of a qualified attorney in preparing a definitive agreement which conforms to the commercial code of the art dealer's state and which forms the basis of a sound business relationship with him.

A number of important contract elements, alternatives, and considerations are discussed below. While they are _not_ a definitive treatment of the artist's legal problems, they cover many of the key issues of his relationship with dealers. They should be further examined and finalized with the aid of the artist's attorney.

What Should the Artist/Dealer Agreement Provide?

1. <u>Who, Where, When?</u> Like any other
contract, the Artist/Dealer Agreement should begin
by identifying the parties and their respective
roles in the agreement as well as the time and place
at which the agreement is to be executed. It is
important that this be done fully and accurately.
One might start with the following paragraph:

> This Agreement is made at_____(city),
>
> _____(county),_____(state),
>
> by and between John Doe, a married man,
>
> hereinafter called the Artist, and the
>
> XYZ Gallery, a Delaware corporation,
>
> hereinafter called the Dealer, to wit:

2. <u>What?</u> The next section should indicate
precisely and completely which functions are to be
performed by each party. Both the artist and the
dealer have many different options. For example:

> The Artist has created and executed
>
> and will create and execute certain
>
> art works in oil/acrylic, on canvas,
>
> in wood/metal, in editions of original

prints, and in a variety of other
media. Such works shall be offered
for sale to collectors, to business
institutions, and to non-profit
institutions,(exclusively, without
reservation/exclusively within a
territory which is described herein/
on a non-exclusive basis)* through
the Dealer, under terms which are
further described herein.
In addition, the Dealer shall perform
certain other tasks in the Artist's
behalf including (but not limited to):

a) Negotiating commission agreements with clients or their representatives
for the creation of works by the Artist,
on the basis of a commission rate
consisting of ____% of the Artist's net fee,
after deducting payments for materials,

----

*Select one term.

supplies and other costs of creating,
fabricating, and installing said works.

b) Arranging and coordinating
the financing of certain art works or
art projects.

c) Arranging, installing, and
publicizing exhibitions of the Artist's
work in the Dealer's gallery (in group
shows/in one-man shows)* at convenient
times, and at least once every ___months,
during the term of this Agreement.

d) Arranging, installing and
publicizing museum and travelling
exhibitions which include or feature
the Artist's works.

e) Promoting the Artist's works
and reputation through the publication
of announcements and advertising
campaigns, and through an active
publicity program, said activities

_____

*Select one term.

to be performed (at the Dealer's sole
expense/on the basis of a mutually
acceptable budget, Dealer to advance
all costs, with both parties sharing
the expenses equally out of the first
proceeds of the sale of the Artist's
work)*

f)   Producing a (brochure/an
illustrated art book/a 16mm. color
film)* within the next___months,
describing and publicizing the Artist
and his work.

g)   Submitting the Artist's work
to no less than_____juried shows and
competitive exhibitions each year for
the full term of this Agreement, at
the Dealer's sole expense. Proceeds
from said activity shall be shared
equally.

_____

*Select one term.

244.

h) Arranging all details associated with lease financing of certain of the Artist's works. Income from such activities shall be lumped with income from regular sales for distribution purposes.

i) Financing and arranging the insuring, framing, crating, and shipping of the Artist's works, said expenses to be charged to the collector at time of purchase, where appropriate.

j) (Extending credit to/arranging credit for)* the purchase of the Artist's works by qualified collectors. Except that no credit will be extended which does not conform to a mutually acceptable written credit policy.

In return, the Artist will:

a) Make (all/all excepting certain/a specific group, detailed in

---

*Select one term.

Exhibit "A" attached hereto)* of his

works now in existence of hereafter

to be executed available to the Dealer

for display and subsequent sale.

b) Cooperate with the Dealer

in the development and execution of

advertising and publicity programs.

c) Pay all costs associated with

maintaining his own studio, creating

and executing his art works, except

as otherwise specifically provided herein.

d) Make sufficient time available

when requested, upon ninety day's

advance notice, to execute to the best

of his ability, certain major commissions

which the Dealer may obtain for him.

e) (Insure his own works/arrange

for insurance by the Dealer)* prior to

shipment to the Dealer.

_____

*Select one term.

f)   Supervise crating and shipment
of works to the Dealer, said crating
and shipping to be accomplished at the
Dealer's expense.

g)   (Refer all prospective clients
within the Dealer's territory to the
Dealer/Accomplish certain sales, paying
a sales commission of ___% to the Dealer,
in such cases)*

3.   How Paid? When? Every contract
provides some consideration which binds the Agreement.
Usually, this consideration is money but, for example,
the act of lending works to a dealer which he has
not purchased might be looked upon as a consideration,
offered in advance, for certain services which that
dealer has promised to perform. Also, the dealer
may provide more than money in payment to the artist.
He may agree to underwrite certain classes of the
artist's expenses or to perform certain services,

_____

*Select one term.

247.

partially in exchange for works. Thus, barter

can constitute a partial consideration. Clauses

treating the problem of payment by the dealer

of expenses and of funds owing to the artist

might read as follows:

a) The Dealer will guarantee to

purchase individual works from the Artist

in the net amount of not less than

$_____per calendar year, based on

a discount of ____% off the established

retail prices of such works. As the

Artist's sales agent, for the purpose

of said purchases, he will have access

to (substantially all/all, excepting

certain/a specific number, as detailed

in Exhibit "A", attached hereto)* of

the Artist's existing inventory of works

and ____% of the Artist's future output,

---

*Select one term.

during the term of this Agreement

at times which shall be mutually

acceptable, but not less than once

every six months.

alternate a) The Dealer will

guarantee an earned income to the

Artist of not less than $_____per

calendar year, based on a commission

rate of fifty percent from the

established retail prices on such works.

Said guaranteed sum shall be paid in

monthly installments, subject to

adjustment twice each year, at the

end of June and at the end of December

at which time any additional earnings

shall be paid or, if sales have not

equalled the guaranteed sum, the Dealer

shall purchase sufficient works from

those in his possession to make up the

deficit. He will have access to

(substantially all/all excepting

certain/a specific number, as detailed

in Exhibit "A", attached hereto)* of

the Artist's existing inventory of

works and ____% of the Artist's future

output during the term of this

Agreement at times which shall be

mutually acceptable, but not less than

once every six months.

b)   In any case, the Dealer will

furnish the Artist at the conclusion

of each quarter with a copy of the

invoices on all works sold, showing

prices paid, the names, and addresses

of collectors and dates of sales.

He will, on request, make available

his financial books and records, and

his inventory records, as well as his

physical inventory, for inspection by

the Artist or his financial representative

to verify the accuracy, timeliness, and

---

*Select one term.

completeness of said reports.

c) The Dealer will bear the full cost of framing, crating, and shipping works left in his care or sold to clients, as well as the full cost of travel, promotion, advertising, mailing, entertainment, entry fees, credit extension, and credit losses related to exhibiting and offering the Artist's works for sale.

alternate c) The Dealer will bear the full cost of framing, crating, and shipping works left in his care, or sold except that when and if previously budgeted costs which were mutually accepted are incurred in relation to promotion, advertising, mailing, and entertainment costs associated with exhibiting and offering the Artist's works for sale, such costs shall be borne equally by

251.

the Dealer and the Artist and shall
be adjusted twice annually in the post-
June and post-December accounting
periods indicated herein.

    d) The Dealer agrees to take out
and keep in force a policy or policies
of insurance for the benefit of the
Artist covering the full wholesale
value of all of the Artist's works
while they are in his custody or that
of his assigns and to pay all the
expenses associated with such insurance
against loss by fire or theft, with
extended coverage.

    4. <u>Who Owns the Works?</u> Whenever the dealer
has actually purchased specific works, it is important
to indicate that ownership of these works resides
with him. This may be accomplished with a properly
prepared Sales Invoice. But, when the dealer has
simply paid an advance against guaranteed sales,
he enjoys an advantage over more casual buyers

since he may thus show a much broader selection of the artist's work. But the ownership of the artist's works should still reside with the artist, and this should be acknowledged in writing. He should protect his rights to remove this property from the dealer's premises, without cause, after proper notice. He might also wish to require that permission be requested by the dealer before such works are removed from the gallery, for whatever reason.

In states which have adopted the Uniform Commercial Code, and in several other states, it will be necessary to record a legal notice with the appropriate state agency indicating the existence of a consignment agreement between the artist and the dealer. Such notices are generally advertised in legal publications to help establish the ownership of the works and to put the dealer's present and future creditors, assignees, and heirs on notice regarding the artist's prior claim to his works. Forms for recording and advertising such claims can usually be obtained at the state agency which handles

the registration of sales financing agreements or
at the offices of any newspaper which deals in
legal notices.

Finally, the agreement should specifically
enjoin the dealer from any action under the terms
of which the artist's works may be assigned or
pledged to some third party as collateral for a loan.
The agreement might read as follows:

a) Unless specifically indicated otherwise,
all the works consigned herein are the
property of the Artist and shall so
remain unless and until they are
individually or severally sold to a
collector by the Dealer acting as the
Artist's agent. Sales shall be made
only on the following conditions:

1) All sales shall be either
for cash or -- if for credit --
only through a valid, properly
endorsed Mastercharge or
Bankamericard.

2) No works shall be removed
from the Dealer's custody except
on the specific written
permission of the Artist or on
the occasion of their purchase.

3) The Artist shall have the
right at any and all times to
enter upon the Dealer's premises
to inventory, audit, and examine
his works and to remove any of
the same.

4) The Dealer holds the Artist's
works herein in trust, and they
shall be returned on demand. The
Dealer has the right to sell the
same for the account of the Artist
at previously established prices,
but the title to any such works
shall always remain with the Artist
until fully paid for. Partial
payment in any form shall be

deemed collateral security only.

5)   The Dealer shall not pledge,
hypothecate, or otherwise encumber
the works herein while they are
in his custody.

6)   (Where required by the Uniform
Commercial Code) the Artist shall
prepare and the Dealer shall
execute an appropriate financing
form indicating the Artist's
property rights in the works
herein and said form shall be
duly filed and advertised at the
Artist's expense.

5.   Sales Territory. As the market for an
artist's work expands, the dealer's normal area of
activity may become too limited for the artist's
needs and opportunities. Anticipating this difficulty,
the agreement should specify the limits of exclusivity
of the dealer's sales territory, to minimize conflict
between different dealers handling the same artist's
work. The agreement might read:

a) The Dealer shall represent the Artist exclusively in the states of New York, New Jersey, Connecticut, and in Eastern Pennsylvania, but he shall make no sales presentations elsewhere. He shall divide his earned (commissions/discounts)* equally with the designated Dealer in any other sales territory in the event that he makes a sale in his gallery to a visiting resident of said territory. However, he shall receive full credit for earned (commissions/discounts)* where the sale is to a resident of his sales territory or to a resident of any unassigned territory.

alternate a) The Dealer shall exclusively represent the Artist in the United States and shall, from time to time,

---

* Select one term.

appoint subsidiary dealers to

operate in various sales territories

to further promote the sale of the

Artist's works. No such subsidiary

dealers shall be appointed without

the prior approval of the Artist,

and each shall represent the Artist

only within his own established sales

territory.

6. <u>Who Sets Prices?</u> The dealer and the artist

should set prices jointly and should decide, in

advance, precisely how they plan to deal with

requests for discounts. Prices should be reviewed

regularly, thus:

a) Exhibit "A", attached hereto and

dated and initialed by the parties herein,

lists the initial works turned over

herewith to the care of the Dealer,

and sets forth the retail selling prices

to be quoted by the Dealer to collectors

and institutions, as well as trade discounts

to be offered to other dealers.
(No other trade discounts will be
permitted/trade discounts of no
more than ____% will be permitted
to bona fide art institutions and
schools)* In the event a trade
discount is authorized by both
parties, the Dealer shall share
the cost of said discount with the
Artist on a pro-rata basis.

b) Prices of all works in the
Dealer's possession shall be reviewed
twice each year, early in July and
early in January. At these times, they
shall be adjusted by mutual agreement
between Artist and Dealer. No interim
price changes are authorized.

c) Prices on works delivered to
the Dealer after the commencement of
this agreement shall be subject to the
same terms and conditions described herein.

_____

*Select one term.

7. <u>Who Pays for Returns?</u> Occasionally, a work
is returned to a dealer for credit. Provision should
be made to adjust the Artist's earned income against
the Dealer's prior or current year's sales commitment
and his commission or discount structure, bearing
in mind the effect of this adjustment on any
guarantees or minimums cited earlier. This
section might read:

     a) The Dealer shall include copies
of credit memos covering returns and
adjustments with his regular periodic
financial report to the Artist.
Previously earned (discounts/commissions)*
and previously reported debits against
advances or credits due will also be
adjusted at this time.

8. <u>How Long Does the Agreement Last?</u> A contract
without a termination date may be ruled invalid. A
clause should be provided indicating that the agreement runs for a specific term such as five years,

---

*Select one term.

subject to cancellation at the end of each calendar
year by either party, on a minimum ninety days'
prior written notice. This section might read:

> a) This Agreement shall commence
> with the present date and continue for
> a period of five years, except that
> either party may cancel this Agreement
> by giving written notice at least
> ninety days prior to the end of any
> calendar year. In this case, the
> Agreement shall be void as of the
> close of said calendar year.

9. <u>How Can Court Fights be Avoided?</u> In order
to minimize costly and time-consuming litigation,
the agreement should provide for arbitration under
the rules of the American Arbitration Association,
in the event that contractual disagreements arise
between the dealer and the artist. This provision
cannot eliminate the possibility of a misunderstanding
or a serious disagreement, but it can reduce the
cost of a legal dispute, often to a fraction of the

cost of a civil court case, and it can expedite
the time required to obtain a decision, which
can otherwise be inordinately long. This section
might read:

a) Any controversy or claim arising

out of this Agreement or the breach

thereof shall be settled by arbitration

in the County of_____

and the State of_____

by and in accordance with the rules

of the American Arbitration Association.

Judgement on the award rendered by the

arbitrator may be entered in the court

of jurisdiction thereof.

10. Verbal Understandings. The agreement
should include a representation to the effect that
no other written or verbal agreements exist outside
the actual contract. Thus:

a) The Agreement herein represents

the entire understanding between the

Artist and the Dealer. There are no

other understandings -- verbal or written --

except as provided specifically herein.